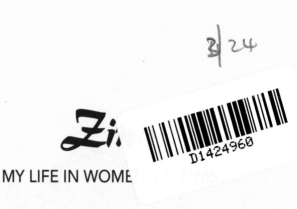

MY LIFE IN WOME

# *Zina*

## MY LIFE IN WOMEN'S TENNIS

# ZINA GARRISON

#### *With* DOUG SMITH

Frog, Ltd.
Berkeley, California

Zina: My Life in Women's Tennis

Published by Frog, Ltd.

Frog, Ltd. books are distributed by
North Atlantic Books
P.O. Box 12327
Berkeley, California 94712

Cover photograph by Carol Newsom
Cover and book design by Paula Morrison

Printed in the United States of America

North Atlantic Books are available through most bookstores. To contact North Atlantic directly, call 800-337-2665 or visit our website at www.northatlanticbooks.com.

Substantial discounts on bulk quantities of North Atlantic books are available to corporations, professional associations, and other organizations. For details and discount information, contact the special sales department at North Atlantic Books.

Library of Congress Cataloging-in-Publication Data

Garrison, Zina, 1963–
    Zina : my life in women's tennis / by Zina Garrison and Doug Smith.
        p.  cm
    ISBN 1-58394-014-6 (alk. paper)
    1. Garrison, Zina, 1963–  2. Tennis players—United States—
Biography.  3. Afro-American women tennis players—Biography.
I. Smith, Doug, 1942–  II. Title.

GV994.G37 A3 2000
796.342'092—dc21
[B]    00-030875

1   2   3   4   5   6   7   8   9 / 05   04   03   02   01

This is for mama ...
who enriched my life with her special love
and, by example, showed me how to share it with others....
And it is for daddy ...
who was gone too soon, yet lingers
still within my heart.

# CONTENTS

# FOREWORD

by
Billie Jean King

ZINA WAS A RISING JUNIOR STAR when I first met her in the late 1970s, but she really didn't grab my attention until she won the Wimbledon Junior title in 1981. Our paths crossed numerous times during the last twenty years. We played against each other before I retired in 1983, and we worked together as commentators for HBO for a couple of years after she retired in 1997. Last year, our bond of friendship grew stronger as we combined our resources to help our country capture major international team tennis titles. Zina was my assistant coach for the 2000 U.S. Fed Cup championship team and for the U.S. Olympic team, which won two gold medals and a bronze medal.

What do I most admire about Zina? Easily, I'd say her generous heart. She shows it by never forgetting the role her family and friends played in launching her career and standing by her side through tough times. She shows it through the time and energy she expends working for the Zina Garrison All-Court Tennis Academy, based in Houston, her hometown. And she shows it through her determination to make life better for those less fortunate wherever they might be. For example, earlier in her career, she created a foundation for the homeless in Houston.

Through her deep religious faith, Zina has managed to overcome various adversities, including racism, divorce, and bulimia. Despite those moments of despair, she continues to move forward, eager to confront new challenges and determined to grow as a human being. I'm convinced that her best years are yet to come.

Thirty years after Althea Gibson broke tennis' color barrier in the 1950s, it was up to Zina to keep the bar raised high for this generation of young African American women striving to be tennis pros. Her success already has helped produce great rewards for African Americans. Venus and Serena Williams say watching Zina on television motivated them. Surely, the sisters' phenomenal success will encourage the next generation to go for it, as well. The more diverse our sport can be, the better it will be. I love it!

And I love having played a role—small though it might have been—in Zina's life story. She, too, has come a long way, traveling on a road peppered with racism, a barrier that I certainly never knew. Like Zina, I'm hoping that one day soon the world community will close that road for good.

Billie Jean King

# Introduction

THROUGHOUT MY CAREER I frequently was asked to explain how a shy, insecure girl from an all-black community in Houston, Texas, grew up to be a top pro in the mostly white tennis world. It wasn't easy. But it was a lot of fun.

Think about it. How many of us get to earn a handsome living playing a kid's game? Moreover, how many of us get to chat and dine with our childhood heroes, become a hero to others, travel overseas, and be recognized as one of the best in the world at your job? Yeah, I know. I've been blessed.

When I reflect on those early years, I realize that it wasn't really that much of a sacrifice for me to have given up a normal childhood for tennis. No one forced me onto a tennis court when I was 10, and no one pushed me to spend nearly every day of my teenage years striving to become a better player. I did it with a smile because I truly loved the game. I lived to play.

It didn't matter to me that tennis was not the game of choice among people in my neighborhood, and I didn't care how many barriers were put in my way. With the Lord's help, I knew I'd find a way to overcome them all.

Althea Gibson and Arthur Ashe, the first black players to win

Grand Slam titles, made my journey less difficult. Althea won the French Open (1956), Wimbledon (1957–58), and the U.S. Open (1957–58); Arthur won the U.S. Open (1968), Australian Open (1970), and Wimbledon (1975). Their trailblazing careers gave me something to aim for; their guidance gave me something to cherish.

Neither Althea nor Arthur ever dwelled on the insults or senseless hatred they endured while trying to play the game they love. I survived some of my own, as you soon will learn.

I loved Althea and Arthur long before I met them, for the things they had done to make it easier for me and other blacks who dreamed of becoming tennis pros. I loved them even more when they touched me personally by showing interest in my development and providing one-on-one help whenever they could.

I was 16 when Althea invited me to join several touring black women pros at her camp in Boston. From the moment we met, I was in awe of her. She had an air of royalty about her. She walked with her shoulders squared and her head held high, her deep, booming voice demanding respect.

Despite our age difference, I've reached the point where I feel comfortable looking upon Althea as a friend. She lives in East Orange, New Jersey, but hasn't been seen in public since suffering a stroke in 1992. Over the years, we've chatted on the phone at least once a month. When I was still on tour, she'd watch me play when my matches were televised and would point out my mistakes.

Hey, that's what friends are for.

She used to tell me I would have been a better player if my serve had been more of a weapon. "You've got to put more pop in your serve," she'd always say.

She still loves to talk about tennis, but every time I ask about her illness, she changes the subject.

I've sent her money from time to time. Those are my dues, and I pay them with pride.

Unfortunately, Althea came along before tennis offered big cash

*Althea Gibson and Arthur Ashe at the USTA Nationals, West Side Tennis Club, Forest Hills, N.Y. Althea was the first African-American to win Wimbledon, in 1967. Photo by Edward Cherry.*

prizes and lucrative endorsements. She remains bitter because she didn't really have the opportunity to make the big money that today's pros earn. I owe the opportunity I received to her.

In my final years on tour, I looked upon Arthur as more of a friend than a mentor. Like Althea, he was an intimidating presence to me. I could never be buddy-buddy with him. I admired Arthur for his warm infectious smile, his self-effacing manner, and his quick mind. We kept in touch by phone and, when we were in the same city, occasionally had dinner. In fact, we were dining—I believe in New York—the night he told me that he had contracted the HIV virus. That happened long before he was forced to announce it in April 1992—a day I won't forget either.

I was playing an event in Amelia Island, Florida, when someone asked me if I had heard about Arthur's news conference. My heart

© Carol Newsom

*Althea, me, and Arthur at Wimbledon in 1990. Althea had come over to London to watch me; Arthur was working for HBO.*

sank when I heard the full details of how he was forced to go public with his medical problem.

When we talked a few months later at the '92 Wimbledon, Arthur didn't mention his health. He was in such high spirits and seemed not to have a care in the world. I figured that if he could be in high spirits under the circumstances, I could too.

He died of pneumonia on February 6, 1993, while I was competing in the Virginia Slims of Chicago. I asked the tournament officials not to schedule me to play on the day of his funeral because I was going to Richmond, Virginia, for the services. When I returned to Chicago, the hot question was why I left in the middle of a tourna-

4

ment. My answer was easy: This great man had cleared a path for me and other future black pros to follow and had achieved so much in his lifetime. The least I could do was go and say, "Goodbye, well done, Arthur."

While Althea and Arthur were inspiring examples for me to follow, another African-American, John Wilkerson, was the key force in both my development and that of another top player—Lori McNeil —my childhood friend. A soft-spoken teaching pro, John sidestepped numerous obstacles and overcame tremendous odds to lead us to the top of the tennis world. Under his tutelage Lori and I became the first African-Americans to reach the Top Ten since Althea and Arthur.

We respected John's down-to-earth approach to life, which included tough-love discipline and religious homilies. He used to tell us that God loves us and that we should love ourselves. Temptation, he said, would be easier to resist if we followed God's teachings. John might have seemed to us at first to be the humble type, but he had fire in his belly. He never backed down when he thought white tennis officials treated us unfairly as juniors or as pros. He made *The Autobiography of Malcolm X* an icon to us before we even understood what it was really about.

John grew up in a little town outside San Antonio. He was, among other things, a cotton picker—and a proud one. He says picking cotton gave him a strong back and made him more determined to move on to a better life.

John taught himself to play tennis when he was 18. In 1971, he won the predominantly black American Tennis Association (ATA) National Championship. Later he moved to Houston and established a year-round junior program. He left his program in 1983 to join me on the tour. A few months later, after Lori also turned pro, John asked Willis Thomas to be his assistant. Though neither man is tall (at 5' 8", Willis is about two inches shorter than John, but a bit stockier), they were giants to us. In terms of personality, they came from the same cookie cutter—quiet but firm.

While growing up, Willis enjoyed playing baseball, football, and basketball. His father had to make him play tennis. "Now, I thank him for doing that," Willis says.

He likes to tell this story about meeting Arthur at an ATA event in Durham, North Carolina, when they were 11 years old:

"He was the No. 1 seed, and I was unknown. I got to the final and had to play him. Before our match, we sat watching the boys' 14s final, which ended in a 26–24 third set. Arthur and I decided we wanted to play a long match, too. He was carrying me the whole match, intentionally missing points when he had game points. So I won the first set 10–8. When we switched sides, Arthur said, 'You know, Willis, you weren't supposed to win the first set.' Then he finished me off 6–0, 6–0.

"We played doubles together for the next three or four years and remained lifelong friends."

When John and I ended our player-coach relationship in 1988, Willis became my sole coach. After that, he worked with me on and off for five years. He once told me he was impressed by the aggressiveness and feistiness I showed when he saw me dominate talented white girls when I was 12. He said he himself was petrified when he faced 12-year-old white boys.

"Zina didn't seem to be nervous at all," he recalled later. "She was just going at 'em. Even in the beginning, she felt that there wasn't a ball that she couldn't reach and return. I knew then that she would be a heck of a player."

For several years during the 1980s, Lori and I were ranked among the top ten players in the world. I have no doubt that our family-like closeness and lifestyle had much to do with our success. Yet, that very success led to distrust and deceit and, ultimately, caused us to go our separate ways for a while.

Lori and I weren't the only blacks to follow in Althea's and Arthur's footsteps. Katrina Adams, MaliVai Washington, and Bryan Shelton were among many others. MaliVai is a fellow former Wimbledon finalist.

6

Aside from winning titles, I've always believed that part of my mission in life was to help other promising black juniors follow in my path. Maybe the next generation of black pros, which includes sister phenoms Venus and Serena Williams, Chanda Rubin, Levar Harper-Griffith, and James Blake, will profit from my experiences and have a smoother road to follow.

I feel compelled to share my life's story, in part because I want to document my linkage not only to Althea and Arthur but the next generation of black pros.

Few black women have become international sports celebrities with an opportunity to see the world as I have seen it. I hope this book will inspire hundreds, maybe thousands of gifted black girls to develop fully their God-given talents, whatever they might be.

Do I have special memories that I can't wait to share with my grand-children?

Lord yes, quite a few. They'll hear stories of my adventures in New York, Paris, London, Toronto, and most of the great cities of the world. I'll tell them about the Times Square-like magic of London's Piccadilly Circus, the cosmopolitan sophistication of Paris' sidewalk cafés, and the semi-controlled chaos in the streets of Tokyo.

"Yes," I'll say to my grandkids proudly. "Grandma's been there, done that many times, many times, child."

This daughter of a Houston postman has spent more time as a world traveler than most Texans, black or white.

During my first few years as a pro, I never thought much about exploring new cities. Every stop those days was strictly business. Once I lost in singles and doubles, it was time to move on, get ready for the next event, wherever it was. I was a portable tennis machine.

But, as the years passed, every city beckoned me to look around, shop, dine out. I had read about historical places such as the Vatican, the great squares and clocktowers of Prague, the windmills of Holland, the Zen temples of Japan, while growing up in my predominantly black community in Houston. I never thought I'd actually get a chance to visit any of them. I figured only super-wealthy people could afford to do that. Suddenly I was there.

The bigger the city, the bigger the thrills. I saw Big Ben in London, surveyed Paris from the top of the Eiffel Tower, and enjoyed moments of serenity within the ancient walls of Notre Dame Cathedral. Simply put, I just took advantage of the opportunities that come with a job that routinely requires international travel.

You know something? I soon realized that by periodically mixing pleasure with business, I played tennis with a more relaxed and productive body and mind.

Hey, I even got to meet the Queen of England! I was captain of the U.S. Wightman Cup team in 1989 when I met Queen Elizabeth II. The Wightman Cup was an annual women's team competition played between the United States and Great Britain. My job was to introduce each team member to the Queen. I was a bit nervous because you're not to speak to her unless she speaks to you first. She did address me, so I got through that okay. I felt like some giant creature in the attention of this little-bitty lady.

I met Princess Di at Wimbledon one year. She was stunning and also quite nice. I don't mean to sound star-struck; it's not that meeting her was so important—she was a measure of how far a little girl from Texas had come.

I never played well on the red clay courts of the French Open, so I usually had more free time in Paris. I spent most of it gazing at the Louvre's centuries-old paintings, some of which took years to complete. For me, the greatest collection of beauty in the world hangs on the walls of the Louvre. It really put my game in perspective. Tennis hadn't evolved when some of these masterpieces were being created.

The Egyptians and early Christians were way beyond my league. But I know when I've met my match. Just to break free of the commercial world and walk in those rooms was another kind of inspiration, a different kind of victory. I may have lost a twentieth-century match, but I won the real game, because tennis got me there.

The show stopper was seeing the Pope. The Italian Open is held in Rome, and tournament officials arranged for some players and staff members to tour the Vatican while the Pope was in town. I'm not Catholic, but I do understand how Catholics feel.

When we entered the church, I felt a strong spiritual presence, and I couldn't wait to see the representative of God. Then the Pope, surrounded by cardinals and priests, strode in. People bowed their heads in prayer. Some cried and trembled. Those sitting in aisle seats extended hands, hoping to touch his robe or to be touched by him. I was suddenly in another world. As he got closer, I impulsively extended my hand. Since I was the darkest person in the church, I figured he had to notice me. I was petrified when he did. He reached over and touched my head—it was like being found by a spirit. Then suddenly I was swarmed by people who wanted to touch me because I had just been touched by the Pope.

I've never felt more blessed, more at peace with myself, than I did at that moment.

Did I learn anything besides tennis during my have-racket, will-travel days on the go? Sure did. Sometimes lessons are clearer when you experience something new in person, instead of just reading about something new. I'll give you a funny example: The first time I took a test in the third grade one of the true or false sentences was: "The concierge will show you the restaurant that's around the corner."

I sat there for a while, trying to figure out, 'What's a concierge?' I learned the answer to that question while staying in a Paris hotel when I played in my first French Open. I was 17. I wanted to know where a department store was and someone suggested that I go downstairs and ask the concierge.

Wimbledon, of course, was "Rome" for a tennis player; it was sacred turf, and everything about it had a special feel. As a young pro, I was tickled by the speech patterns and wry humor of British television commentators. I also used to love to hear the commentators and some

9

of the older former pros talk of sensing the ghosts of former champions past scampering about on Wimbledon's fabled Centre Court. I knew all the great tennis champions had played there, but I was never intimidated by history. In fact, when I defeated two-time Wimbledon champion Evonne Goolagong in the fourth round in 1982, my rookie year, it was the first match I ever played on Centre Court, but it was home.

Evonne, an Australian Aborigine, also happened to be one of my all-time favorite players. I am sure my attraction to her was influenced by the fact that she too was a woman of color, bucking the odds to succeed in a mostly white sport. When I was a young junior player, I remember watching Evonne on television and realizing that, even though she was Australian, her skin was dark like mine. Sometimes at the park, we'd try to hit a topspin lob or a slice backhand, have a little twist in our walk or sit down cute, like Evonne. You go through that kind of stuff when you see people you admire on television.

Aborigines have their own language and tribal traditions, and are, in many ways, similar to Native Americans. Evonne was raised in Barellan, a small farming village of about nine hundred people. At the urging of tennis coach Vic Edwards, she moved 360 miles to Sydney.

With her brown skin, dark brown eyes, and swift, easy movements, Evonne was one of the most graceful tennis players I'd ever seen. She was so exciting and feminine to watch, since she seemed to glide across the court, her feet never touching the ground. She won ninety-two titles, including six Grand Slam crowns, in her sixteen-year career.

Besides being an Aborigine, Evonne was special for another reason. She won her first Wimbledon title in 1971 and later, after marrying Roger Cawley and having two children, she returned to the tour and made history in 1980 by becoming the first mother to win Wimbledon, beating Chris Evert 6–1, 7–6 in the final. Now that's impressive!

However, none of that mattered when I met Evonne on Centre

Court in 1982. I thought only of the many sacrifices mama and others had made to get me there. I didn't care who I was playing; I was going to try to win the match. As usual, I relied on my quickness and instincts. I moved Evonne from side to side and attacked every short ball that she hit. By keeping my eyes focused on the ball, I never dared take a glimpse at the figure I was so in awe of on TV. I think it helped that I was a newcomer and she knew nothing about my game. But it also helped that she was on the downside of her career and not as hungry to win as she was during her earlier years. I know that now, partly because I frequently lacked that go-for-every-shot ambition when I felt my own days were numbered.

After beating Evonne, I felt no remorse, but I left the court with an even greater admiration for her. She was nice when she greeted me before the match and, after she lost, she was just as nice. That's the kind of person she was, and she hasn't changed. To me, that's the mark of a true champion.

After that victory, I always felt that Centre Court was my personal playground. Beating Evonne and reaching the '82 Wimbledon fourth round in my rookie year are high on my "most memorable moments" list. I reached the Wimbledon semifinals in 1985 and the quarterfinals in 1988. But in my book my rookie year accomplishment topped those achievements.

I won my first title—the 1984 European indoors in Zurich, Switzerland—two years after turning pro. That title was especially important to me because, with it, I became the first black woman to take a tour event since Leslie Allen won Detroit in 1981.

I won the European Indoors again in 1985. I also got my first tour win against Chris Evert that year at Amelia Island. My most memorable and emotional battle against Chris occurred in the 1989 U.S. Open quarterfinals. That was Chris' final match as a pro.

I talked beforehand on the phone to Willis about the strategy I should use. He told me not to try to serve-and-volley her off the court. He said, "Use your speed to run down everything she hits."

Chris led 5–2 in the first set, but I rallied to win 7–6, 6–2. Chris was No. 4 in the world at the time, so, when I got behind, I decided I had nothing to lose and relaxed. I liked to play Chris because she didn't have any great physical weapons. She had a steady baseline game and played smart all the time. I always felt I could hang in there with her strokes, but I knew I could never coast and think I could outlast her from the baseline. In our U.S. Open match I just tried to keep her in an athletic position. I used a variety of spins and angled shots, keeping her off-balance. Each time she hit her feeble second serve, I closed into the net, then placed the ball in the corner away from her. I had watched Martina beat Chris with a similar strategy many times.

I never felt good about that victory, mainly because I knew I would be remembered as the player who beat Chris in her last tour event. Don't ask why, but I felt like a traitor.

When the match ended, Chris gave me a hug at the net. That made it a little better, but I started crying anyway. One newspaper actually referred to me as a villain. Everybody loved Chris.

Undoubtedly, she was among the best I'd ever seen. Her rivalry in the 1980s with Martina Navratilova stirred interest in women's tennis and attracted millions of people to the game. Even during the years that Martina dominated the tour, you never could count Chris out when she played her. And they were fun to watch. You saw a clash of two different games, played by women with totally different lifestyles. Their confrontations surely will be remembered as one of the great sports rivalries of all time.

Nothing and nobody rattled Chris Evert. She always looked cool and in control. You never saw her sweat, and I mean that literally. I used to think: How could she be out there in the hot sun running around and not sweat? Chris never believed anybody could beat her. You could look at her and see that she wasn't a phenomenal athlete. But mentally she was as tough as a piece of beef jerky.

Although we didn't hang together that much when we were playing on the tour, I remember her being extremely funny. She'd often have a group of players cracking up when she was telling clean or dirty jokes. Her dirty jokes, of course, were really raunchy.

Lori and I were 16-year-old kids in Houston when we first saw Chris play. We chased her for about an hour, trying to get autographs. I admired her so much as a player and, as I got to know her, I respected her even more as a person.

A few years ago, Chris and I were at a U.S. Open booth, supporting former pro Leslie Allen, an African-American, who was trying to find blood donors for her baby daughter. Leslie's child needed bone-marrow transfusions. Chris and her husband, Andy Mill, have three children, so Chris understood what Leslie was going through and wanted to help.

A white lady asked Chris, "What is the difference between white blood and black blood?"

Chris snapped at the woman, "Blood is blood!" The she looked at me with eyes that said, 'Why would she even ask that question?'

Chris didn't see Leslie's baby as a black child. She saw her as a person who was sick and needed help. This may be obvious, but it was an emotionally uplifting moment for me because Chris did it so naturally. She didn't make a point to impress me. In her and my world we were already way past such prejudice even if the world at large hadn't caught up.

Because of Chris' girl-next-door image, most crowds pulled for her to win wherever she played. I faced my only hostile crowd in Worcester, Massachusetts, about a month after I had beaten Chris. In my first match I noticed that nobody was clapping for my good shots. At an indoor event, you can really tell what the crowd is feeling. I couldn't figure it out because I thought I was playing really good tennis. I got the same reaction in my next match. Then I realized that the crowd was upset because I had beaten Chris a month ago in her final match.

As proud as I am of what I have accomplished during my fifteen-year career, I realize that I'm still pretty much a footnote or less in black communities. Consider this: Though I was an internationally acclaimed tennis pro, my performance at the 1988 Seoul Olympics is what made me a superstar in my neighborhood. That's a fact. Most black kids don't care about who's who in tennis. But when you come home an Olympic champion, you're hot stuff.

During the Olympics I got to meet several athletes, including boxers Roy Jones and Riddick Bowe. I later saw them fight as amateurs! I trained with Jackie Joyner-Kersee whom I had met earlier at the Women's Sports Foundation. Before then, I was so naive, like a child. I used to think all you had to do on a track was run with all your might. I didn't understand that your arms and legs had to work a certain way and I didn't know about different breathing techniques. The Olympic track stars teased me a lot when I first got on the track.

I had no skills and not a clue about running. I'm sure my butt looked like two basketballs!

I never got to the point where I could call myself an actual sprinter or racer, but I did get to where they stopped laughing at me.

Now let me tell you about Zina, the Houston girl, at the Olympics:

At the '88 Games Pam Shriver and I represented the USA in tennis. It was an eye-opening experience for both of us. Basically, we were two young women who had by-passed college for the pro tour. We had to get used to dormitory life, eating in cafeterias, and being around all those real athletes with beautifully sculpted bodies.

Pam and I shared a room. She's a non-sleeper, and I can sleep through anything. She told me I was a great roommate because it was like I was never there. I called home one day, and my sister Clara said they saw me snoring on television. Pam had videotaped proof of my napping skill!

Pam and I represented the USA in both singles and doubles. Pam and Martina Navratilova were probably the best women's doubles team ever to play the game. They won twenty Grand Slam doubles titles, including the 1984 Grand Slam itself, which means they won the Australian Open, French Open, Wimbledon, and U.S. Open that

*Wendy Trumball, me, Mary Carillo, and Pam Shriver at the West Palm Beach, Florida racetrack where we raced Formula One cars at a Philip Morris invitational tennis event.*

year. They also hold the record for most consecutive doubles match wins at 109. Obviously, I felt great about playing dubs with someone carrying that kind of portfolio.

Pam's best performance in singles at a Grand Slam event occurred in 1978 when at age 16 she reached the U.S. Open final, where she lost to Chris Evert 7–6, 6–4. Pam overcame limited athletic ability with unbelievable determination and hard work. She was considered a scary opponent when her serve-and-volley game was solid.

We had to play against each other in the quarterfinals. The winner was assured of receiving a bronze medal in singles. (At the '96 Atlanta Games, the semifinalists met in a playoff for the bronze medal.) Pam and I had gotten along quite well, but we both wanted that bronze. The night before our match, I left the Olympic Village to stay with my brother, Rodney. During the match, I heard Rodney yelling, "Come on, Nanny; you can do it, Nanny!" He had always called me Nanny for some reason. That got me psyched and I played really well, besting Pam 6–3, 6–2.

I lost to Steffi in the semifinals. Then she beat Gabriela Sabatini 6–3, 6–3 in the final. Later, Pam and I teamed up to win gold medals, defeating Jana Novotna and Helena Sukova 4–6, 6–2, 10–8 in the final. We lost five match points while I was serving at 9–8. Two of those match points were double faults. That didn't make me feel good. My hands were shaking on every point. It really was very nerve-wracking. We clinched the gold on the sixth match point when Novotna hit a return of serve long.

I don't think I fully understood what we had done until they put the gold medal around my neck while were standing on the podium. Pam started crying when the national anthem was played and I was like 'Wow!'

One thing's for sure: In my neighborhood, Zina the Olympic gold medalist was a bigger star than Zina the tennis champion would ever be.

Yet I assure you my journey hasn't been pain-free. I've certainly had my share of sadness and heartache to overcome. My father and an older brother died before I got to know them. My mother died shortly after I turned pro. It's scary when you lose the people who you knew loved you just for being you. After my mother died, I felt a loneliness, an emptiness that was hard to shake. I constantly tried to fill it with food. Through therapy I learned that my parents' death, combined with my low self-esteem, were contributing factors to my bouts with bulimia, an eating disorder I still struggle to control.

I was never comfortable with the way I looked, especially when I compared myself to the trim white girls on tour. For more than three years I threw up every day, hoping to alter an image of ugliness I saw when I looked in the mirror at my naked body. That basketball butt was no joke.

The ups and downs, the joy and sadness of my life were all relived within the framework of my fortnight to remember—1990 Wimbledon. That's when I reached my one and only Grand Slam singles final and enjoyed the most satisfying moment of my pro career. A round-by-round account of my Wimbledon '90 matches seems an appropriate backdrop for the unveiling of my story, since my life changed so dramatically after those two weeks. Before Wimbledon began, I was just a top tennis player. A fortnight later—like a caterpillar turning into a butterfly—I felt like I had sprouted the wings of a superstar. An instantaneous three-year clothing and shoe endorsement deal with Reebok was among the most significant goodies I received. I never looked back.

Finally I began putting this book together in 1996, a year in which injuries and heartache conspired to disrupt my life. My troubles actually began a year earlier when I learned that my husband at the time, Willard Jackson, was having an affair with a girlfriend of mine. It's tough to focus on your forehand when life gives you a backhand slap like that.

I suffered first-round losses at seven consecutive events before beating Nathalie Tauziat 2–6, 6–3, 6–4 at the Advanta Championships in Philadelphia in November 1996. A shoulder injury forced me to default the next round, so I ended my fourteenth and final year on tour in both physical and emotional pain. Willard and I were divorced in the fall of '97. As you will learn, I'm still sorting through these events and setting the course of my life as a retired tennis pro.

My dream of dreams is to raise children in a loving family relationship. Ideally, the good Lord will continue to give me all the courage and strength I need to carry on and keep becoming a better person.

I've often felt blessed and burdened simultaneously. At times I've wanted to escape the pressures attached to being a role model and gifted athlete. Other times I felt the need to pinch myself just to be sure that I really was who I was and that I was really doing what I was doing. Sometimes, I still wonder if my life as a star tennis pro was real or if everything that happened was some kind of weird dream inside a dream.

*Me at two years*

*Me at four years*

# 1

# Tumorlina

W HEN I WAS A CHILD, I never envisioned myself as a tennis
player, but I did have visions.

I was three years old when I saw my father lying in
the bed with my mother and me. I saw him even though my father
had died of a stroke when I wasn't quite six months, not even old
enough to realize who he was. I used to see this man walking around
in our house, but no one else could see him. I'm sure it was my father,
watching over me. I was able to describe him to my mother without
ever having seen any pictures of him. I can't recall having visions of
any other person but my father.

I remember walking through the house when it was real dark
and saying, "Well, Daddy is here and we're playing." It was really
strange. My father was a U.S. postal worker, a mail carrier who was
loved and admired by the 361 families on his route. I'm told that
whenever he missed a day, some of them always would ask about
him.

In a tribute that appeared in the *Houston Chronicle,* one patron
said this about my father:

"As new families moved in, he always made a point of stopping
to talk to them and personally seeing to it that their mail was for-

warded. And the children just loved him. He patronized all their soft drink stands in the neighborhood. We used to tell him to save his money, but he would always say, 'Now, Ma'am, you know I got to keep my kids in business.'"

My four sisters and my brother, Rodney, used to get scared when I talked about seeing and playing with "the man in the house." Once, when I was sitting in a car with my sister Clara, I saw my father walking around the car. I asked Clara if she saw him.

"What? There's no man walking around the car."

I said, "Yes, there is; it's daddy."

Clara jumped out of the car and ran to mama yelling, "That girl's out there seeing things again!"

Rodney used to call me the "Vision Girl."

I envied my sisters and brothers so much because they got to do something I never did: touch our father. I felt like a part of my life was missing because I never got a chance to play with him, hug him, or kiss him goodnight. Everyone else in my neighborhood had a father. The way my father died so young, it was like we were supposed to accept it and move on. Yet not having a father from the beginning was, without a doubt, one of the most painful realities of my life.

As I grew older, instead of having visions, I had premonitions. Sometimes I was able to foretell death, illness, and good fortune. I correctly predicted the sexes of each of my nieces and nephews. I remember my mother taking me to see a spirit lady who said that sometimes the seventh child born in a family has "the vision" or is born with a veil, an extraworldly aura.

I've also been told that the devil tries to keep the seventh child from coming into this world, so I feel blessed just to be here.

Zina Lynna Garrison was indeed Ulysses and Mary Elizabeth Garrison's seventh child, born ten years after her sister, Althea. Mama named me Zina to let my father and the world know that I was the final one. She had had A through Z, so she was done. There were several other Zinas in my high school, so I can't say it was an uncommon name. My middle name, Lynna, was original. Mama thought of the name Lynn and added an A.

Since I came ten years after Althea, it's safe to say that my parents weren't exactly expecting me. Concerned about a swelling in her abdomen, my mother, who was then 42, went to see a doctor. He told her that she would need an operation to remove a tumor. Lucky for me, she got a second opinion. I joined the Garrison clan on November 16, 1963. Naturally, my parents took a ribbing for having another child so late in their lives.

My sister Clara told mama, "I can't believe you and daddy are still doing that! How could you let this happen to us?"

And, of course, everyone thought the "accident" should have an appropriate nickname. So they called me Tumorlina.

My brother Willie was the first-born in our family. My twin sisters, Judy and Julia, came next. I think it's true what they say about twins: they do share a special closeness. Sometimes my twin sisters can blow your mind when you hear them talk. One twin will start a sentence and the other one will finish it. They're a trip.

After the twins, Clara, Rodney, and Althea arrived in that order. Althea was the baby before I came along.

My father was only 43 when he died. About six months later, Willie also passed away. I was so young at the time that I have no memory of my brother. That is, I have no memory actually—just of people talking about him, so he seems real to me.

Willie was an outstanding athlete. He liked baseball best and was good enough to be a catcher in the Milwaukee Braves' minor league system. One day, when he was playing shortstop, a ball took a bad hop and hit him in the left eye. A tumor developed, and doctors had to remove his eye. Then the eye became infected. All of a sudden, what seemed to be a non-life-threatening injury turned fatal. Willie was 21 when he died.

People always talk about how great an athlete my brother Willie was. I think about him a lot. Supposedly he would have gone on and played in the show. My brother Rodney had lots of stories about what our life would have been like if Willie had lived. Willie was the oldest and I was the youngest, and he probably would have taken care of the rest of us. Then I might have been even more of a spoiled brat. Hold on there; I'm just kidding—at least partly.

Recently a skycap at the airport told me about watching my brother play baseball. The way he talked I truly wonder how good Willie might have been—Ken Griffey, Jr., Derek Jeter, who knows? It would have taken a lot of the weight off me, but then would my life have gone into tennis? Maybe. Maybe not. It's an interesting scenario. Things turn out the way they do for a reason.

In the mid-1960s my family moved from Ft. Worth to Sunnyside Garden, an all-black, working-class neighborhood just south of downtown Houston. We lived in a three-bedroom house with a garage that was converted into a fourth bedroom. Our address was 9306 Noel. The house was on a huge corner lot, between a side street and an empty lot. Our lot was one of the biggest in the neighborhood, plenty of grass too; my brother and I never liked to mow it. There were a couple of small trees in the middle, but it was mostly a big open space. Our yard served as the neighborhood hangout. We played volleyball, baseball, kickball, and other games there. We'd string up the volleyball net between two of the trees. It was like a playground and meeting place for neighborhood kids. Mama and her friends, and my friends and I, frequently gathered there for games and talk. Kids shortcut through our lot on the way to the elementary school, which was right down the street. They left a little trail, like an Indian path.

Our corner yard was like a magic place; then the rest of the neighborhood began out from there. There was a small apartment complex next door and a park across the street.

A church around the corner used to have "Commodity Day" about twice a month. Cheese, butter, peanut butter, and sometimes meat were among the foods given to church members with large families. Mama would get stuff; then she'd make me get in line to get extra cheese. When you're growing up in an environment in which you at least have food and a roof over your head, you don't think that you're poor. I saw people who were a lot poorer than we were. I used to hate it when my mother made me stand in those long lines to get free cheese.

Roxie Johnson used to make her kids do it, too. Ms. Roxie, a former nurse, was one of mama's best friends. She and her three children lived down the street from us. Sometimes when mama, who was a diabetic, slipped into a coma, I'd race down the street to get Ms. Roxie. Winos in the park across the street knew something was wrong at my house whenever they saw me running to get Ms. Roxie.

Ms. Roxie was a topnotch cook. In fact, she ran a bootleg hamburger shop and sold candy in her garage. Bus drivers would stop the bus in front of her house to get one of Ms. Roxie's hamburgers. On weekends, there were long lines of folk waiting to bite into her sizzling patties. I used to be a regular customer in that line.

Actually, I was both a cook and a customer. When the line got pretty long, I'd help grill the burgers. I didn't mind donating time because Ms. Roxie would always stop and come running whenever mama needed help.

By the time my father died, the twins were college seniors, getting ready to be on their own; Clara was just starting college; Rodney was in the Army; and Althea and I were the only ones at home with mama and my grandmother. Her name was Julia Walls, but we called her "Granny" after the grandmother on the television show, "The Beverly Hillbillies." Granny never missed that show.

Mama was a nurse's aide but didn't work very much after I came along. She was sick an awful lot. Granny did all the cooking and housework. Mama said my father did the cooking when he was alive. She said he used to make the best pancakes from scratch with flour and water. He also loved to barbecue. My brother Rodney took up

*My grandmothers, Dahlia Garrison and Julia Stinston Walls, Ft. Worth, Texas, in the '70s.*

where my father left off in the cooking department. Rodney's barbecue is to die for.

Granny was in charge of discipline. If you did something wrong, she'd send you outside to get the switch she would use to whip your butt. I could never figure that situation out. It must have been the way her parents did it when she was growing up. She'd chase us around the house and run us under the bed, then wait until we had to come out. Granny also was the one who got everyone to go to church. We attended Jones Memorial Methodist Church, and I was just a baby when I was baptized there.

Even though she wasn't a regular church-goer, mama taught me to believe in God, trust Him, and read the Bible. While Granny took us to church, mama watched religious services on television every Sunday. Granny also helped me understand the difference between right and wrong and taught me to hold onto my spiritual beliefs.

Some of my friends attended the neighborhood Baptist church. Our services were quiet compared to services there. I could not understand people shouting and getting happy in church. Every time I went, I wondered what was happening.

Many years later, I attended services with my husband Willard at his church in Denton, Texas, just outside Dallas. People at his church also shouted and ran up and down the aisle.

I think we all spoiled mama because she was sickly. We wouldn't let her do too much housework. I actually slept with mama until I was 15, and I'm sure it was because I had lost my father at such a young age. I was so afraid I was going to lose mama, too.

My sister Althea used to tease me all the time about being a big baby in the bed with her mama. Althea used to get everything her way, and everybody made a fuss over her. She was "the baby" before I came along. I'm sure she was jealous of me then. But I didn't care. Mama was like a comfort zone for me. Still, I did break away from her apron skirt every now and then to engage in adventures that most young kids enjoy.

When I was nine, I hung around with a girl who lived around the corner from us. Her name was Zina too; her last name was Stoneham. We did the tadpole scene together. We'd put tadpoles into jars and watch 'em grow legs and turn into frogs. We also dug crawfish out of ditches. We were the neighborhood tomboys, the only two girls who liked to play softball and basketball with the guys.

After my father died, our family managed to get by with funds we received from his life insurance. But whenever funds got low, my older sisters, my brother, and other family members made sure that mama, Granny, and I got whatever we needed. Our family always stuck together. Whatever I needed, I got it from someone in the family—uncles, aunts, godparents, or someone else. But we were by no means rich. I only got the things that I really needed, like clothes, shoes, and lunch money.

Because of tennis I grew up quickly and, when it was my turn, I took on the role of family elder. Throughout most of my career, I made sure that at least one family member got to see me play at each major event. All my sisters and Rodney have been to the French Open, Wimbledon, or the U.S. Open at least once.

None of them came to London to see my 1990 Wimbledon matches, but they were with me in spirit and pulling for me on every shot.

# 2

# Fortnight to Remember, Round 1

## *Garrison vs. Samantha Smith*

WAS COOKIN' when I reached the Wimbledon final in 1990, and I'm
not talking just about the way I played tennis.

Every morning I served a breakfast fit for a famished football
team: bacon, sausage or ham, with eggs, pancakes, grits, and sometimes oatmeal. I began each day with a stack of pancakes because
that's my favorite meal. At night the menu consisted mainly of a vari-
ation of well-seasoned chicken with lots of veggies.

I sprinkled my meats with Lawry's Season-All because I couldn't
always find the spices or vegetables I needed while shopping at the
closest jolly-ole-England Safeway or a little market around the corner from our rental in Wimbledon Village. Yeah, I did the grocery
shopping, too. I was shopping all the time because I didn't want to
be mad with anyone else for forgetting to pick up something I really
wanted.

Why would I, Zina Garrison, the fifth-ranked player in the world,
spend so much time in the kitchen cooking for a group of men while
I was competing in the world's premier tennis event? Because cooking relaxes me. And because my support group included my husband

Willard, who loved to start the day big. He wouldn't eat breakfast unless it included some kind of greasy meat. I could never understand how he could eat the biggest breakfasts and stay so little!

My agent was shocked when he came over one night and found me in the kitchen cooking for everybody. Oprah Winfrey's cookbook had just come out, and someone had bought a copy for me. I was trying her recipe for baked french fries and oven-fried chicken.

I began my run for the world's most prestigious tennis crown facing Samantha Smith, a British pro who was ranked No. 143 in the world. I was the No. 5 seed, behind No. 1 Steffi Graf, No. 2 Martina Navratilova, No. 3 Monica Seles, and No. 4 Gabriela Sabatini. While I was never completely comfortable with the role of celebrity, I was shamelessly pleased and proud to see my name right up there with the world's best women pros.

We rented a house in Wimbledon Village within walking distance of the All England Lawn Tennis & Croquet Club where the matches were played. Willard and I shared the two-story cottage with my coach, Sherwood Stewart, and trainer, Vincent Moses. There were three bedrooms, a living room, kitchen, and den.

To me, the area around Wimbledon is similar to many wealthy suburban communities in the United States, although the homes there might be older and the landscaping more quaint. Most top players rent places near the courts because they expect to be there for the full two weeks. Plus, it relieves the players of non-tennis concerns, like fighting traffic to get to your match on time. More importantly, being in a house—instead of a hotel—helps you feel at home.

We had a really huge movie rental bill during that fortnight because we'd rent at least two movies every evening from a video shop around the corner.

I insisted on cooking breakfast and dinner every day. Everyone except me ate lunch at the courts. I'd get smoked turkey from the deli and make turkey sandwiches to carry to the court.

Some people called my support group "Zina's entourage." I don't think so. Neither cheerleaders nor freeloaders were allowed to join Team Garrison. Each member had a job to do, and each task was essential. Team Garrison's mission: get Zina prepared mentally, physically, and emotionally to win major tennis titles.

Willard handled all logistical concerns, including airline travel and hotel accommodations. He also briefed me on the pros and cons of possible business ventures. Willard was always a pretty shrewd businessman. He was the first man I knew who played motivational tapes instead of music while driving. He loved Anthony Robbins.

Robbins is a motivational speaker and personal coach. People listened to his tapes back then because he was very uplifting, very positive, all the time. Willard liked that. It didn't do much for me.

Vincent, my trainer for that entire year, kept me strong and fit. He pretty much told me what to eat and what not to, when to jog or lift weights, and when to go to bed. Going to bed was never a problem for me. I was ready for bed every night at 9:30. Still, you wouldn't be wrong to say that, though I was 26, Vincent acted as my baby-sitter.

Sherwood arranged my daily practice sessions, scouted my opponents, and devised tactics and strategies for each match. A fellow Texan who resided in Goose Creek, he was an All-American at Lamar University. He won fifty-four men's doubles titles, including two French Opens (1976, 1982) and an Australian Open (1984), during a twenty-year pro career. He reached a career high ranking of No. 60 in singles and No. 4 in doubles. Sherwood and I actually won the 1987 Australian Open and 1988 Wimbledon mixed doubles titles.

My scout was overjoyed when our names were added, as former champions, to the walls of the players' dining room at Wimbledon.

"The one thing about the wall," he often said, "is that your name will be up there even when you're gone."

I'm not sure why we jelled as doubles partners. It certainly wasn't because we had similar personalities. Maybe we jelled as partners because of our opposite attitudes. On the court, Sherwood was emotionally erratic. Generally, he was kind of calm, but occasionally he'd explode when we got a bad call. I was pretty even-tempered, never got flustered.

I wanted Sherwood to coach me because he knew so much about the game. This is not to knock John or Willis, but they never played on the tour; Sherwood did. I felt that he could relate better to what I was feeling because he'd been there. He expressed his thoughts in easy-to-understand terms. Plus, he knew I was a moody person. When I was in one of my negative moods and challenged everything he said, he gave me some distance. I suppose I was comfortable with him because I knew there was no game-playing or emotional baggage attached to his words.

Sherwood was the only white member of Team Garrison at that time, but he never seemed uncomfortable walking through Wimbledon Village with the brothers and sister.

The night before my first Wimbledon match, I prepared the evening meal as if it were the most important thing I would do all week. A dash of salt here, a pinch of garlic there—I tasted this, stirred that, and moved around the kitchen with the confidence of a master chef. I was finding some rhythm.

I served Italian chicken with broccoli and mashed potatoes. Staying busy in the kitchen cooled out my mind. If you're a top seed, you are expected to win—if not all the time, most of the time. And no excuses! Friends and family members put pressure on you often without realizing it. You wouldn't believe the number of times in Houston I've gone on a court emotionally drained from scrambling around trying to make sure that all my family members had tickets to my matches.

Yet I realized that friends, family, and the black community-at-large were a special catalyst that, at times, drove me beyond my usual reach. After upsetting Jimmy Connors in the 1975 Wimbledon final, Arthur Ashe spoke of being inspired not just by the Centre Court fans, who routinely root for the underdog, but by the prayers of millions of black supporters who vicariously shared his victory.

Wimbledon is the ultimate proving ground for most players. Anyone who knows anything about tennis has heard stories of drama-
filled clashes on Wimbledon's fabled Centre Court. I've had a special
feeling for the prestigious grass court event ever since I won the Wimbledon Junior crown in 1981, my first year playing there.

The two-week event is held each year at a 13½-acre renowned
grass court facility, which is hidden by a mixture of tall hedges, flowing ivy and other shrubbery, and fencing. A golf course sits directly
across the street from the All England Club's main gates. With its
rich history and intimate setting, Wimbledon is the game's most dramatic venue and grandest prize.

How is Wimbledon different from all other tennis events? Let
me count the ways:

(1) It is the only major sport event that makes some of its prime
seats available on a first-come, first-serve basis. Every year, hundreds
of fans "queue up" as the Brits say, or stand in line, to buy tickets at
the gate. People from not only greater London but other European
cities camp outside the gate, sometimes for several days. They come
with sleeping bags, tents, blankets, and pillows. I was always impressed
by their friendly spirit and orderly lines. I can't imagine the same
thing happening in the States because I know that at least one person would try to break the line. There is a limited number of seats
on the main-show courts, which include Centre Court and Court
No. 1. Several thousand "grounds passes" also are available each day,
but unfortunately they aren't good for entrance into the show courts.

(2) If you're not wearing a predominantly white outfit, you don't
play on those hallowed courts. Period. Here again, Wimbledon is the
only major tennis event that has such a strict dress code. I think most
players accept it, and some high-profile players use it to their advantage. Andre Agassi is among several top pros who launch new clothing lines at Wimbledon each year. The late Ted Tinling, who was a
liaison to the women's tour when it was sponsored by the Virginia
Slims, caused a stir in 1949 when he designed Gussy Moran's outfit
with colored lace panties. Wimbledon banned Tinling's creations,

and the all-white attire rule at Grand Slam events stayed in effect until the USTA allowed colored clothing to be worn at the U.S. Open in 1972.

(3) If a member of Great Britain's royal family is seated in Centre Court's Royal Box, protocol requires the women players to stop at the service line, turn, and curtsy; the men, as they walk onto the court, must stop, turn, and bow. I was always nervous about doing that because I thought it would be embarrassing to curtsy using the wrong foot. I doubt if anybody would have cared.

The Royal Box used to freak me out because you're there with your opponent, trying to act like you're not nervous, but knowing you got a bunch of butterflies flapping around inside. However, Queen Elizabeth last appeared in the Box in 1977, the year Great Britain's Virginia Wade won the title.

(4) Starting play on Centre Court is at precisely 2 P.M.

(5) Strawberries & Cream are sold in the stands.

(6) A grand finale dance—the Wimbledon Ball—honors the champions on Sunday night.

Wimbledon brings out the best in you as a player. I know that I was psyched to excel whenever I stepped on any of those perfectly trimmed grass courts. I adored feeling the grass under my shoes, and whenever I played on one of the outside courts, I loved being close to the crowd.

Grass courts also favor players who are quick and aggressive, and that was my style. Three of my fourteen career titles were won at grass-court events. Those include Birmingham, England, twice (1990 and 1995) and Newport, Rhode Island, in 1989.

I don't believe I have ever been as confident and composed as I was for my first-round match against Samantha Smith. That year, before each match, I sat in a corner to get myself mentally and emotionally prepared. Sometimes I read books, but mainly I listened to music on my Walkman. Before major events, I often listened to rhythm &

blues, gospel, and other music with soul-stirring melodies. I also chose songs that made me feel like I was on a beach. I liked listening to the waves crashing on the shore and the seagulls flying overhead. I'm an emotional player, so I don't want to be too keyed up before a match.

When I played Samantha in the first round, I doused my soul with an hour's worth of gospel music by the Winans: *"Ain't no need to worry what the night is going to bring/It'll all be over in the morning."*

I found it relaxing before each of my subsequent matches to listen to the Winans sing. It was uplifting and spiritual. I once met them at a function that followed the Essence Image Awards, and I thanked them for getting me to the final of Wimbledon in 1990. It was a surprise and a blessing to get to tell them in person.

It didn't take me long to shake the jitters that come with every first-round match. My serve was on and I had no trouble breaking hers. Nothing personal, Samantha, but it's not always easy to be ruthless when you know your opponent isn't strong enough to beat you. Your mind fades in and out, and sometimes you unintentionally ease up when victory seems within your reach. As a top-ranked pro, I knew that bad things can happen at major events when you lose your focus —so I kept my eyes on the prize. After I took care of Samantha, 6–2, 6–1, my mind moved to a more pressing problem: what to fix for dinner. Everyone enjoyed my first night's offering, so naturally I wanted to make sure the next meal would be as good, if not better.

# 3

# Love That "Sissy" Sport

"C onfessions of a Tomboy" would have worked just as well as
a title for this chapter.

That's what I was, without a doubt. Every summer, the
city sponsored Little League softball and baseball games at the park
directly across from my house. When I was eight, I was talented
enough to play on a team in a division with girls aged 14 and 15. This
was softball, fast pitch. I pitched and played shortstop; I was pretty
good at both positions. One game I started out at shortstop and then
ended up finishing as the closer.

I liked the shortstop position because that's where a lot of the
action was, and you pretty much ended up controlling the game. I
was very good at ground balls. I am basically low to the ground. I
move like a cat stalking mice, so balls come right into my glove.

I also seemed to be able to make the right play at the right time,
throw to the right base to get the lead runner, and double runners
off. I never perfected the double play before I became more a pitcher.
I threw a nice fastball. Nothing else. No change, no curve. Even
though Rodney showed me the two-fingers-out grip, I said, "No way.
I just want to throw it as fast as I can." My tactic was: aggressive,
aggressive, aggressive. Go right at them. Total strikeouts. Ryan express,

baby; "Here it is, hit it!" That's God's scouting report on Zina, any game, any life situation.

I have good reflexes, hand to eye. I got so I could hit the baseball on a line just about every time. I was never one to go up there and try to wham a home run. I always tried to find a little soft spot within the other team. Then I would use my speed to get a couple of extra bases. I was a right-handed hitter, and I could pretty much control the ball—right field, left field, hand-eye coordination, put it where you want. I guess I was a tennis girl in the making.

When I watch baseball now, I don't think about home runs; I look for where that empty space among the fielders is going to be.

I was pretty fast on my feet, too. In fact, I never lost a race running against girls my age. My brother Rodney got me to compete in boys' events, and I ran away from them, too. Not long ago, Rodney reminded me that Greg Anderson, an NBA guard, was one of the boys his little sister used to wipe out.

In elementary school we had field days at the end of the year. There were sock hops where you'd get in a potato bag and other crazy stuff. And then came the real thing: sprints and relays. I was always the fastest. It felt as though I were running through air, fast as I can, faster, faster, low to the ground. That was Zina at her happiest.

I felt free.

I never accepted the training part of it, though. I just liked to run. Kick my shoes off and go barefoot. I don't like things under my feet. I like the feel of the ground. Grip, move, stay down.

I much preferred short-distance running—fifty, sixty-yard dashes, no more than a hundred meters. My legs are short and powerful. I wear down easily on longer runs. My thighs would be burning. My wind was, like, I'm going to die. Short is quick bursts; you feel the pain and it's over. You're there.

Deborah Edwards, a sprinter at the 1972 Olympic Games, lived in our neighborhood. Sometimes Deborah ran laps around the park, and Rodney said I'd trot along behind her like I was an Olympic track star, too.

Rodney didn't mind me tagging along with him to the park or anywhere else. He taught me to play every sport and treated me not like an annoying sister but a sidekick, the little brother he didn't have. I guess that's why the bond between us is so strong.

I was nine years old when I was named "Queen" of the parks and got my picture in the newspaper. I really felt like I was big stuff then. Cocky was too mild a word to use to describe me. My sisters used to call me "the kid with a bad 'tude." I truly believed I could beat anybody in any sport I played. I wasn't afraid to go up against anybody. My motto was: whatever it takes. It can be done if I put my mind to it. It *is* possible.

I think often about the long road I have traveled to reach this point in my life and how grateful I am to those who helped make it possible. My brother Rodney, for example, never tried to suppress my desires to be an athlete and never coaxed me to stay home and play with dolls. Lord knows what my life would have been like if Rodney hadn't decided that his little sister might be good at smacking tennis balls back and forth across a net.

Rodney played baseball for Texas Southern University during the time I was his companion. He practiced on a field in MacGregor Park, close to the tennis courts. When I was ten, I used to help Rodney get ready for games by shagging balls and playing catch with him on the sidelines. Carol Middleton, who was Rodney's girlfriend then, happened to play tennis. That's probably the only reason Rodney even knew where the courts were.

One day he told John, the park's tennis instructor, that he had a little sister who played baseball, ran track, and would probably be a player. John asked him to bring me by the courts so he could see for himself what I could do.

A couple of weeks later, Rodney dropped me off but didn't tell John I was there. It was a warm and pretty Sunday afternoon, and nearly everyone seemed engrossed in some form of athletic competition. I sat on a bench about twenty feet from the action, watching John hit balls across the net to another player. They were both sweating a lot. I had no idea what tennis was all about because I had never seen anyone play it. Of course, it took me only a few minutes to say to myself, 'That ain't much. I can do that.'

A ball rolled into the grass directly in front of me. As he was retrieving it, John stopped and stared at me; he was probably thinking, 'Who is this strange little girl?' He asked, "What are you doing here?"

I didn't respond; not a word. I didn't even move my lips.

Then John said, "So you're just using up God's air."

I shot right back, "It's my air, too."

He smiled.

When he learned that I was Rodney's sister, he asked me to wait around until he finished the lesson. When he returned, he said, "So you want to play tennis."

I told him, "I don't know how, but it looks pretty easy."

He put a racket in my hand and led me to the court. Obviously, I knew nothing about how to grip or swing a racket. I thought you were supposed to hit a tennis ball like you hit a baseball. So on my first swing, I smacked the ball far over the fence. I expected to be complimented, but John was just laughing at me.

He told me the object of the game was to keep the ball *inside* the lines on the court. 'Okay,' I thought, 'I can do that, too. Plunk it over second in front of the right fielder. At least a double if I tear. If they bobble, I got a triple or more.'

After I got the point I struck the ball with a smoother swing and more control. I think John was pleasantly surprised because I consistently and aggressively stung the ball across the net inside the lines. Whatever it takes....

Though I didn't have great form, every ball he hit to me went right back at him just as hard. I'm a quick learner.

When Rodney came to pick me up, John told him to enroll me

in the beginners program that met every Thursday. He promised me if I improved, I could come every day. That was fine with me. It was something I could look forward to doing.

I went to the beginners program for a month. I stopped attending during the Christmas season because Santa brought me a new bicycle that year. All I wanted to do then was cruise with my friends. Nobody in my neighborhood cared about tennis anyway. The kids from Sunnyside did basketball, football, baseball, and they ran track. Tennis was totally foreign. When I started taking lessons, my friends would tease me and ask, "Why are you playing that sissy sport?"

Bike-riding took the place of tennis for a good three and a half months. My brother lured me back to the courts when he learned that comedian Bill Cosby would be there to participate in a clinic. Rodney wanted me to get a chance to meet Cosby and, if I was lucky, hit a few balls with him. I was indeed lucky because that's exactly what happened. I hit with Cosby and shot the ball right back at him.

This time I was hooked; tennis captured my spirit. I made a total commitment to learn to play the game. From then on, I rarely missed a day on the courts. I became a fixture in John's junior program. I never wanted to go home. During the summers, I'd stay all day and start crying when Rodney or Althea came to pick me up after dark.

"We couldn't understand how she could go out there at eight in the morning," Rodney said, "and when we would go pick her up at eight in the evening, she still wasn't ready to come."

Althea remembered (when it was her turn to pick me up) having to "knock me upside my head" a couple times to get me to go home.

After a while I was just considered to be weird. None of my friends could understand why I spent so much time playing tennis.

Consider this. One day we stayed in the park as Houston flooded. The water rose so high we almost got trapped in the pro shop. I certainly couldn't go home, but we made it to Lori's house (you'll hear more about her in a minute or two); she lived on higher ground not too far from the park. The next morning maybe no one else was thinking tennis, but *my* first question was: "When can we go to the courts?"

Even though sections of Houston had been damaged by a major flood, I was all set to hit balls.

After graduating from Texas Southern, John became the head teaching pro at MacGregor. He played tennis there, too. Mostly whites were signed at MacGregor then. That was the time of the tennis boom sparked by the popularity of USA superstars Jimmy Connors and Chris Evert. Despite the boom, not many blacks were interested in tennis.

John said, "When I first got there, MacGregor had mostly a white clientele. We had only one black junior in the city playing junior events. I wanted to get more black people playing. I figured I could do that by starting a kids' program. Our college team was pretty well known in Houston, so when I got the job, black people started coming there."

Lori McNeil, daughter of the late Charlie McNeil, an NFL defensive standout for the San Diego Chargers, joined a month after I did. We were a month apart age-wise. I was born in November, she in December. Actually, Lori began playing a bit earlier because her mom had played tennis with her before she started going to John. Lori and I were ten when we became best friends. We played doubles together and always shared a room when we traveled. There were only four girls in the program when we joined.

Recalling our early friendship, Lori said, "It was something that just happened from the first day we met. Before I knew it, seven years later, I was traveling all over the world with the same person."

There's no doubt that we pushed each other in the juniors. We remained close during the early days of our pro careers, but the friendship suffered after she signed with International Management Group (IMG), a major sports firm, in 1989. I'll always think of Lori as a sister, but that split hurt our friendship for quite a while. More about it all later.

I spent nearly every free moment at the park. Nothing mattered more than tennis. Sometimes mama worried about me being away from home after dark. But most of the time, I think she was glad that she didn't have to worry about me getting into any trouble. She always knew where she could find me. John said the program was like a free day-care center for the parents and, looking back, I think that's exactly what it was. It also provided me with unexpected lessons in arithmetic.

It took me a while even to care about keeping score. All I wanted to do was whack that ball again and again and keep it inside the lines. When I played a match, I knew I had to be winning as long as I didn't make an error before my opponent did.

John and his assistants didn't realize that I couldn't keep score until I played my first tournament. Then everybody found out I didn't have a clue. One Saturday, a group of kids from MacGregor played a group from another park. All the other matches ended within an hour, but mine lasted for more than three hours. After each point, whether I was serving or receiving, I'd wait for my opponent to move to a side of the court, then I'd go to the other side. Edgar Arnold, one of John's assistants, came on court and asked me what the score was. I answered by crying. I was too embarrassed to tell him I didn't know. I just assumed I wasn't losing.

Years later, Edgar said, "They played that match for nearly four hours until the other girl just finally couldn't go on any more and walked to the net and shook Zina's hand. That was the funniest thing I had ever seen."

Reminded of the incident, John said, "We didn't realize that Zina was having problems with the scoring system, and she had an opponent who took advantage of this. Right before they finally stopped, a lady came over and told us that our little girl won the match forty-five minutes ago, but the other little girl kept the game going because Zina didn't know how to keep score. Zina played for a long time without knowing how to score her points."

I finally learned to keep score by thinking of it as my personal rap song with a chorus of "Love, 15, 30, 40, game." By the way, "love" is zero in tennis scoring. I'd sing it again and again until I knew it by heart. Eventually, I also learned what deuce games, deuce points, and advantage points meant.

Here's the way it works. If you start out as server and win the first point, you lead 15–0. Fifteen is for the server, zero for the person who received the serve. Since zero is "love" in tennis, the score would be announced 15–love. If you win the next point, it's 30–love, 40–love if you win the third point; if you win four straight points, or four points before the other person gets three, then the game is over. On the other hand, if the receiver wins the first point, the score is 0–15. And so on.

A tie of 40–40 means the score is deuced. When that happens, a player must win by two more points. One more point for you breaks the deuce, but you need another to end the game in your favor. If your opponent scores next before you, guess what: it's deuce again. Six games wins a set ... unless it's 5–5; then you need two to win, just like points in a game. 6–5 doesn't end the set; 7–5 or some other, higher combination does. Kind of confusing to the non-tennis playing world, and it certainly had my young mind boggled.

Then there's the twelve-point tiebreaker, which is played when the set score is tied at 6–6. In a tiebreaker, the first player to get seven points in the thirteenth game wins the set. However, if the score is tied at 6–6, a player must win two consecutive points before claiming the set.

Learning to keep score probably was the toughest thing about tennis I had to do. Everything else was pretty simple, fun, and straightforward.

Right from the beginning I choked up on the racket head. That's something people remember me by because it's a habit I was never able to break. Playing tennis was like playing ping-pong with a smooth, fluid stroke that came right from the waist, starting in the back and going to the front. When the ball hits the strings, I'm in control of the direction that ball's going to go.

Now, a tennis ball is a strange thing. It's not what it seems to be. At first glance, anyone can see it's made of rubber, about the size of a hardball, and has felt on the outside, sort of compounded together.

But court surfaces apply different degrees of pressure to the ball and change its density. A hard court gives a little less pressure, a clay court a little more.

The ball also changes size. When I'm playing well, in the zone, the felt-covered rubber circle seems the size of a basketball; when I'm not playing well, it's the size of a golf ball.

When you connect with the ball, it's effortless—"fluent" I sometimes call it, though I know that's not quite the right word. The ball seems light, not like an object at all. I want to say it feels featherless, but I actually mean it feels feathery. It's just energy. The ball is nothing; it's air.

When you're not playing well, it feels like hitting lead, like a rock from your hand all the way up to your shoulder. You're trying to muscle it.

So this weird little unimpressive rubber toy filled with air can be either feathers or lead, a basketball or a golf ball; it all depends on your fluidity and confidence.

My strings, from the time I was 12 years old until the time I retired, were made of real gut—what people call catgut. It's not really cat's guts because that would be horrifying. It's synthetic fibers. When you're playing well, the sound of the ball hitting in the center, the sweet spot, is a ping, like music: *Piiiing!*

I love hitting a tennis ball, period. I especially love volleying indoors because you can actually hear the sound. It's like a composition of notes never played before. You hear the music of yourself playing.

When you're not playing well, the ball hits at the top or the bottom of the racket and it's a very dull sound.

The tennis court itself is a boundary, and you control it by the racket and your mind. I learned that very early, in my body, before I even fully understood it. When you've played as long as I have now, you pretty much place the ball where you want.

John said, "Always keep your head watching the ball from the moment it hits the racket." So I had to learn the court and its different angles from the ball, not from the line. If I make contact at a certain point of my body, the ball is going to go one place. If I make contact at another point, it's going to go another. That's how the lines become almost invisible after a while.

The lines on the court are not target marks that I aim at or inside of. Instead, I hit the ball by touch, and know when I contact it whether it's going to be in or out. Looking at the result is not necessary; I can feel the placement in the hit. The lines on the court turn into the racket and stroke, the position of my hands and feet; it's not a map outside of me.

I find that, if I'm confident within the moment, I can put the ball just on the right side of the line. My confidence tells me it's going there. You don't actually visualize the line so much as you visualize the ball and yourself being on the court. You know where the court is on the other side, so you don't need lines.

Location comes from hitting the sweet spot, feeling good, being in the zone, in control. That ball tells you when it leaves your racket whether it's going to be in or out.

If you're right-handed, you always try to hit the ball out in front of your left leg—the opposite if you're left-handed. Each time you try to find that sweet spot; you find it not just in the racket but in your legs, the arc of your stroke, your mind.

When the opposing player hits the ball, I always know whether it is going in or out, particularly when I am at the net. I judge it by the trajectory of the ball against my height. Some people are better at that than I am.

I knew if a ball was traveling just a little bit above my head, nine times out of ten that shot was going to go out. Little landmarks like that become second nature.

Lori McNeil was always great at knowing the trajectory of the ball—she did ten out of ten. Somehow she knew even if her opponent's ball was going to go out by just a hair. You could tell she knew because she didn't move and it would sail just beyond the line.

Lobs were always my best shot. You run back and hit the ball as high as you can, trying to land it as close to the baseline as possible. Topspin was very hard for me to learn. My aggressive lob with topspin I actually learned from watching Andre Agassi at the U.S. Open one year. I'm naturally a very flat hitter. I have to come from under the ball and brush up on it to get the spin.

The thirty juniors in John's program trained during the week after school from 4 P.M. to 7 P.M. and from 8 A.M. 'til dusk on the weekends. Every day we did some stretching exercises and ran sprints and laps followed by a couple of hours of hitting drills on the court. We usually ended our day running the dreaded bayou.

What's the bayou?

Several inlet-type bodies of water run through the city of Houston to Galveston Bay. The bayou is a major one that ends up at the ship channel, carrying sewage the length of Houston. I think the water is in the process of being purified. Some days it smells real bad; other days you can look down and see fifty million happy catfish.

That bayou can be pure torture if you don't have a strong mind and body. On a hot summer day—which is nearly every summer day in Houston—running its course was like racing in a sauna. Nothing was tougher, and those who could do it knew they were in good shape. Plus, if you couldn't run the bayou, you couldn't hang.

We also had our own training ground right in the middle of Mac-Gregor Park. There was a 250-yard oval-shaped jogging path encircling several clusters of trees—a few hundred or so.

After drills, John had us run around those clusters of trees twenty-five times. But I'd always go around them fifty times. When they told us to do ten sprints after running the bayou, I'd do twenty. Whatever they made the group do, I'd double it.

Parents hoping to push their kids toward a pro career often ask me what age their kids should be enrolled in a rigorous junior program. I tell them only: when the kid wants to do it, not when the parents want them to. Thank goodness mama didn't know anything about tennis and never wanted to learn anything about it. My devotion to tennis was mine alone.

To be a top pro, a child has to give up a large chunk of his or her childhood. Nearly all of my spare time was spent learning a new stroke, perfecting the strokes I already knew, or learning to play with greater discipline and focus. When I say that I played tennis every day from age 11 to 18, that's only a slight exaggeration. There are no shortcuts.

I reached the final of my first tournament by winning just one match. Did I mention there were only four players in my division? A minor detail. I got a trophy, too.

Within a year, John had us playing in USTA events throughout Texas.

I remember meeting a top-ranked white player named Nancy Talley in one of the first USTA 14-and-under events I played. Ranked No. 1 in Texas, Nancy hadn't lost a match that year. She beat me pretty badly. A month later, we met again. John was just hoping I would be respectable and not get blown away again. I not only beat her, I dominated her. Nancy got me the first time because I was nervous about playing the top junior in Texas. She faced a calm and determined Zina in our rematch.

John said he knew then that I was a gifted player. He understood that I hated to lose, and he was right about that. After beating Nancy, I didn't lose a junior match in Texas for the next five years. I went to the Texas regionals one year and only lost four or five games. I was ranked No. 1 in Texas most of the time, while Lori was usually in the top five. I had tougher battles fighting politics and racism off the court than I did in most of my matches on the court.

*Lori McNeil and I receive trophies at the ATA National Championship Junior Division, 1978, in Princeton, New Jersey. Lori became the #9 player in the world in the late '80s. Photo by Edward Cherry.*

John taught us tennis. He never dealt openly with the racial issue. But if you're black and growing up in Texas, you're having to deal with it every day. I maybe didn't know about the politics, but racism was easy to spot.

John always taught us to use race as a positive. I mean, we're different, but that's something to appreciate. We all have different cultures, and we have different things to teach and learn from each other. Race shouldn't be a negative thing. But it's kind of imbedded into our foundation and gets carried over to the next generation of children and then their children's children. It almost doesn't matter whether they have their own opinions about it or not. People don't know why they think the way they do. An attitude just gets passed down. To me, racism is the worst kind of hatred because it's so cruel and senseless.

All we really wanted to do was play tennis, and we never looked at people the way they looked at us. But many white tennis parents and officials didn't take kindly to their kids getting beat consistently by a couple of black girls from a public park. When I started playing USTA events, I was 11 years old, stood 5' 3", and weighed about 115 pounds. Once I started beating the white girls, tournament officials began saying I was too big and that I was lying about my age. They demanded that my mother show my birth certificate every time I played. John totally lost it about that.

He said, "I told them to let me see the birth certificates of all the other kids. They claimed I couldn't request that. I said, 'If you can, I can.' That's so insulting. Either they were saying we're too ignorant to read a birth certificate or we were lying. So I just put it back on them and it stopped."

That was the first time I realized that we were not just playing tennis but, by winning, we were blacks stepping on a lot of toes in a white sport. Things really got nasty when Lori and I became Texas' best junior girls. When we went to Dallas to play the Texas sectionals, one of our chaperones was in the area where the draw was being made. She heard them say, "Throw all those niggers in the same bracket."

Sure enough, they put all the black players in the same bracket. We were pretty hot about that. Of course, they denied collusion. They claimed we got in the same bracket due to the luck of the draw.

They didn't want John's program to succeed, and they definitely didn't want me to be the best that Texas had to offer.

Years later, John recalled the situation: "Zina was a big target, and there was a feeling that if you beat Zina, you have beaten our program. So Zina was like a big trophy. Every time she played she was under the gun, but she took the pressure well because she was so competitive. Most of the time, it was just a matter of how many games she would let them have."

48

The other black juniors from MacGregor Park and I never felt wanted or comfortable socially at Texas events, but we enjoyed playing the ATA, a predominantly black national tennis group that was formed in 1916 by a group of black doctors, college professors, and businessmen. Back then, blacks were not allowed to join white country clubs and couldn't play in public parks or in USTA-sanctioned events. So a few interested black professionals established their own clubs and conducted their own tournaments. The first ATA national championship was held at Druid Hill Park in Baltimore, Maryland, in 1917.

The ATA was the main training ground for both Althea Gibson and Arthur Ashe. Dr. R. Walter Johnson, a black physician who had a tennis court in his backyard in Lynchburg, Virginia, played a key role in helping Althea break the racial barriers in the early 1950s. Althea was educated and trained to be a world-class player mainly through the efforts of two black physicians—Dr. Johnson and Dr. Hubert Eaton, of Wilmington, North Carolina. Each summer, Althea trained at Dr. Johnson's home and traveled around the country with him, competing in ATA events. During the school year, she stayed with Dr. Eaton, finished high school in Wilmington, and moved on to Florida A&M where she earned a degree in physical education. Althea's autobiography, *I Always Wanted to Be Somebody,* was dedicated to those two doctors.

Thanks to their generosity and support, in September 1950, Althea became the first African-American to play in the U.S. Open, then known as the U.S. Nationals. It was held at the West Side Tennis Club in Forest Hills, New York. Earlier that year, the same club had barred the renowned Dr. Ralph Bunche, Jr., and his son from membership because of their color. As a diplomat for the United Nations, Dr. Bunche had negotiated a cease-fire in the Mideast and in 1950 became the first African-American to win the Nobel Peace Prize. Yet he couldn't play tennis at Forest Hills.

Althea won her first-round match in the 1950 U.S. Nationals, but lost to No. 3 seed Louise Brough 6–1, 3–6, 9–7 in a rain-interrupted second-round match. In an interview years later, Bertram Baker, who was then the ATA's executive secretary, noted that the audience was as foul as the weather.

"Fans were shouting from the stands for Althea's opponent to beat the nigger, beat the nigger," said Baker. "I'll always remember it as the day the gods got angry. A flash of lightning came and knocked down a statue of an eagle on the stadium court. The rain caused the match to be postponed, and the next day Althea lost three straight games and the match."

After Althea's debut, Dr. Johnson organized the ATA's Junior Development Program. His goal was to nurture a black junior who would be good enough to win the Interscholastic Championships held each year in Charlottesville, Virginia. Over a twenty-year period, hundreds of talented black boys and girls from across the country trained on Johnson's backyard court and spent summer months playing ATA and USTA junior events.

Arthur Ashe was ten years old when he arrived at Johnson's home. Eight years later, Arthur fulfilled Dr. Johnson's dream by winning the Interscholastic Singles Championship in 1961.

The ATA junior program was similar to the program that John created in Houston. We too trained year-round and traveled all over the country to play in ATA and USTA tournaments.

John took me to play in my first ATA nationals in San Diego in 1975. My mother and other parents sold barbecue dinners to raise money for the trip (later I paid for other such trips that way). We rode in a big chartered bus. It was my first long trip on a bus, my first time playing in a national tournament, and it was great fun. John and Edgar said I was as happy as a little kid let loose in a candy store.

I remember getting there and seeing for the first time all these black kids who looked just like me. I never realized that there were so many black people from all parts of the country playing tennis. I sprained my ankle shortly after I got there, and John barred me from attending a party for the juniors. But I just had to go. Sure enough,

*Being presented the ATA National Championship trophy by Rev. Houston, President of the ATA. I won all three events in ages 14, 16, and 18. Photo by Edward Cherry.*

I was in there, getting down, dancing and hopping around on one foot with Willis Thomas III when John came in. He was furious!

He reminded me of the many sacrifices that my family and other people in Houston had made to send us there. He told me that they would be very disappointed if they knew that I was risking further injury by dancing on a sprained ankle. I was angry at the time, but I came to understand that tennis and partying didn't go together. John's lecture also helped me realize that if I was going to be serious about becoming a top competitor, I needed to be as disciplined off the court as I was on the court.

He didn't say it, but I knew that if I didn't get more focused and serious-minded, I wouldn't get to travel to any other ATA events.

When I was 14, I won the 1977 ATA National Girls 18s title, played in Princeton, New Jersey. A few years later, I met one of my closest friends, Katrina Adams, at an ATA event in Detroit. Katrina, who grew up in Chicago, now lives in Houston. She reached the Wimbledon fourth round in 1988, her rookie year on tour. She was among the handful of black pros at Wimbledon in 1990 and became a trusted confidante as well as one of my favorite shopping companions.

Before I start reminiscing and gossiping, I'd better get back to the story line.

# 4

# Fortnight to Remember, Round 2

## *Garrison vs. Cecelia Dahlman*

T'S FUN SEEING SMILES OF CONTENTMENT on the faces of people you've just fed.

My friends call me the black Martha Stewart because I like throwing different types of parties and entertainment. I'm the one who's always coordinating things, putting the menu together, and coming up with themes and activities.

All my sisters can cook, but my brother Rodney is the best in the family with meats. Mama didn't cook, but my granny was extra-good. She prepared meals professionally for a wealthy family that lived in downtown Houston.

Besides a variety of chicken dishes, I also like to make turkey lasagna and different kinds of pasta. Cajun dishes are my favorite, so I decided that we'd have gumbo at least once during the first week of Wimbledon. To celebrate my first-round victory against Samantha Smith, I opted to serve chicken burritos with Spanish rice and refried red beans and chips. I got hungry just thinking about it.

Actually, I was hungrier to do well against Sweden's Cecelia Dahlman, then No. 73 in the world, in my second-round match. Though I had never played Dahlman and didn't know much about her style of play, I was pretty confident and relaxed. But not cocky. Like I said earlier, I was cookin' on the court, too.

Permit me now to give you Zina's recipe for success on a tennis court.

Speed, undoubtedly, was the main ingredient that helped me reach the top. I used my speed to the max; it was something I always worked on and realized was an asset. But I've always believed that my stubbornness and determination kept me there. I never gave up, regardless of how far behind I was in a match or how badly I played. I always believed I could win. Just don't lose another point. That has been my attitude ever since I first learned to play. I want to win every point, every game, every time; I run the court like a gazelle stalking its prey.

I never allowed the fact that I was short, pigeon-toed, and black to stop me from doing anything. It didn't matter to me who was on the other side of the net. I always attacked the ball. I was relentless not by strategy but by nature.

I liked to move my opponents around, putting them in positions where they had to show athletic excellence. If they lacked speed or agility, they were dead meat against me. My ability to quickly analyze and find flaws in my opponent's game was one of my major strengths. Usually I knew how to exploit a player's weakness after watching her play just a couple of games. People never talked about me being a smart and savvy player, but I was.

My forehand crosscourt was my favorite shot. If I hit it cleanly and on a sharp angle, my opponent's return—if there was a return—usually would be short. That allowed me to move toward the net and smack a forehand down-the-line winner.

Remember I mentioned topspin when discussing my lobs? John taught me how to hit a shot in which the racket is swept under and then through the ball. You must have a good follow-through in order for topspin to be effective. On a hard surface, topspin causes the ball to jump—or kick upward—when it lands. Sweden's Bjørn Borg won Wimbledon five times and the French Open six times by hitting nothing but topspin from either side.

As I told you, my groundstrokes are very flat and I hit them deep, aiming for the corners. Like most American pros, I learned to play on hard surfaces. Many European and South American players learn to play on clay, a soft surface that doesn't allow balls hit with topspin to bounce as high as they do on hard surfaces. Balls hit with heavy topspin should be returned while they're still rising. Andre Agassi is among the best at doing that.

I had one of the best drop shots in the game. I loved to slide the racket under the ball, applying underspin, then watch my opponent scramble to the net to return the finessed placement. I used drop shots a lot because most women players just aren't quick enough to reach a short ball. Women pros generally prefer to play from the baseline.

My backhand-down-the-line was my best shot when I was a junior. On key points, I'd occasionally run around my forehand to hit my topspin backhand. Arthur used to compliment me on my topspin backhand, but he'd always add, "You've got to learn the slice backhand, too." So I did.

To hit an effective slice shot, you must slide the racket beneath the ball while moving your weight through the ball. In my later years, I hit mostly slice backhands and rarely hit topspin ones.

Tommy Ray Scott, one of John's aides at MacGregor Park, taught me how to hit overheads. Scottie trained us to use an extended finger to follow the flight of the ball as it left our opponent's racket, staying focused on it as it declines. He taught us to always take the ball while it was in the air, never let it drop. If a ball hit the ground, we'd have to run extra laps or do twenty push-ups. We hit tons and tons of overheads every day. Lori was the best at hitting overheads. When we got on tour, all of us thought our overhead shot was far better than any opponent's.

Basically, a player is either a serve-and-volleyer or a baseliner. A third type might be called an in-betweener, one who does some of both. Billie Jean King, Martina Navratilova, Pete Sampras, and John

McEnroe are among the game's best serve-and-volleyers. A serve-and-volleyer usually moves toward the net after each serve and tries to end the point quickly with put-away volleys.

Baseliners prefer to win points by outslugging their opponents from the baseline. In order to beat the good serve-and-volleyers, a baseliner must go for the lines, angling the ball away from the net-charging volleyer. That's called "hitting passing shots." Monica Seles, Agassi, Borg, Jimmy Connors, and Steffi Graf are among the game's best baseliners.

Throw me in with the baseliners, although at times, I was an in-betweener. John taught me the volley; Willis refined it when I worked with him. Sherwood and Angel Lopez really worked me until volleying became a strength. Sportswriters occasionally said they couldn't figure out my playing style, and I couldn't always figure it out myself! The fact is, some days I could be a very aggressive player; and other days I was more of a counter-puncher, waiting for things to happen. I think a lot of it has to do with my personality and what's going on in my life. My game reflected so much. I'm moody, and sometimes I felt confident and aggressive, and sometimes I felt better staying on the baseline and waiting.

I generally stayed away from the net because I had a yukky serve. My service was like powder-puff. It had no pace on it. If I had to play myself, that would be the thing I would attack. My second serve would kind of sit up there like a watermelon balloon—people used to tease me about Zina's two-mile-an-hour serve. My serve would sometimes hang around for days. But in tennis a slow ball can be the hardest thing to hit because it leaves you too much time. I actually got a lot of points off my second serve because it was so soft that people weren't ready for it. It was like a knuckleball—no pace to measure.

I think being 5' 4" inhibited me from ever having a huge serve, but my serve definitely could have been better. Actually, being a coach now is teaching me a few new things about my own game, technique-wise. Billie Jean King recently taught me some techniques and tips for my serve.

As a junior, I won all the time without having a strong serve, so I felt I didn't need one. No one forced me to improve my serve. I used to dismiss any attempt by my coaches to make me practice serving by saying my arm was sore. Sherwood was the only coach who wouldn't let me get away with that excuse. He made me serve every day regardless. His insistence paid off for me at the '90 Wimbledon.

Most players need a vigorous warm-up to determine how well they're going to play when their match starts. Not me. As long as I'm feeling good mentally—no matter how I look in practice—I know I'm going to hit the ball solid and with a good rhythm when play begins at a tournament. If I look really good in practice, I get nervous in my match. Image might be everything with Agassi, but with me, attitude is everything. It's all about attitude and the way I feel. And against Cecelia Dahlman, I felt absolutely marvelous: "Love, 15, 30, 40, game."

I beat her 6–2, 6–1; it was the same score I posted against Samantha Smith in the first round. Dahlman, who's a bit more than six feet tall, was a serve-and-volleyer, but not very quick. I beat her to the net most of the time and didn't give her much of a chance to play an attacking game. When she did get to the net, I stroked forehand or backhand passing shots down either line and cross court.

Whenever I play Wimbledon, I figure the best way to sharpen my singles game is to enter doubles and mixed doubles. That way, I get to spend much more match-play time on grass courts. The women's tour consists of more than fifty events; at least three—Wimbledon, Eastbourne, England, and Birmingham, England—are played on grass. Most players want and need more time to adjust to a slick, uneven surface, which causes erratic bounces.

Moreover, playing doubles makes me more aware of my need to be aggressive in singles. While I don't have a big serve that's productive to follow to the net, I'm pretty quick. I knew I couldn't win against the top players if I didn't attack the net and play a serve-and-volley game.

My solid singles play put me in the right frame of mind for doubles, which usually starts on Wednesday of the first week. Since I was playing all three events—singles, doubles, and mixed doubles— I didn't spend much time on the practice courts those first few days. I teamed up for women's doubles with Patty Fendick and mixed doubles with Rickey Leach.

I reached the second round in all three events, so I knew I had to pace myself. I was in excellent shape and confident. I felt good about everything and was stroking the ball with authority. Despite the extra matches, fatigue wasn't a factor. I can't recall ever losing a match because of stamina—that is, until I got an eating disorder. Even as a junior, I was always able to go the distance. Running those extra laps around the bayou got me through a lot of tough encounters, as a junior and as a pro, especially in extreme heat. Whenever I played a strong opponent and felt a little bit tired from the heat, I'd think back and say to myself, 'I ran the Houston bayou in 100-degree heat, so I can stay here with you! And I will—as long as it takes for me to walk off with balls in my hand. Win!'

On a grass court, luck sometimes determines who wins a close match. Bad luck can get you bounced out of a match that you knew you couldn't lose. To keep the goblins and bad vibes away, you sometimes have to do things that might seem a tad silly, maybe even nutty. Am I superstitious? Can Michael Jackson do a baaaaad moonwalk? You bet I'm superstitious. Most players are.

I think Mary Joe Fernandez might be the worst at trying to ward off bad luck. Even when she's practicing, Mary Joe won't step on a line on the court. When we played doubles together, I found myself avoiding every line that she avoided. I wasn't going to be outdone. I was doing loony stuff like that as a rookie pro.

My towel had to be folded the same way during every match. Even now, when I'm traveling on a plane, my seat belt has to be pulled a certain number of times when I buckle up. I hate flying, anyway.

Sherwood thought I was a bit wacky with all my superstitious ways during the '90 Wimbledon. On the second day, I made him park in the same spot that we had for my first-round singles victory.

Each day, I made my adopted godparents, Al and Velma Nellum, sit in the same seats to watch me play. I was just as fanatic about avoiding bad-luck spots and demons that might have been lurking in the streets of London or Wimbledon Village.

Whether we were in London, in the Village, or at Wimbledon, I never allowed the group to split up when approaching a light pole, telephone pole, or bus-stop pole. Naturally, no one was allowed to walk under a stepladder. I went to bed each night between 9:30 and 10 P.M., not a minute sooner or later. Indeed, it was a ritual I wouldn't dare change, regardless of how nutty some thought it was.

Sherwood didn't allow my superstitious ways to stop him from giving me the information I needed to do my best whenever I played. At night before each singles match Sherwood and I got together and discussed a game plan and made notes about what I needed to do on court for the next person that I was to play. If he didn't know much about my opponent, he'd talk to other coaches and find out as much as he could. Before and after each match, we'd go over my opponent's strengths and weaknesses. I was like a sponge at those sessions, soaking up everything Sherwood had to report.

When I look back and think about all the time I spent learning different strategies, tactics, and nuances of tennis, I can't help but wish that I had been as studious and determined in my elementary and high-school classrooms. Unfortunately, if my report card showed all Cs, I was happy. I should have convinced myself that inattentiveness in class or failure to do my homework might lead to seven years of bad luck. As superstitious as I was, maybe that might have jump-started my brain cells.

# 5

# My School Days

I T'S TOUGH GOING THROUGH SCHOOL behind a trouble-maker sibling. The teachers think they know what to expect so they label you right away.

I attended B.H. Grimes Elementary, which was just down the street from my house. The Garrisons had made a name for themselves at that place long before I got there. My brother Rodney was remembered as a saint who could do no wrong. Althea, on the other hand, was the devil's little helper. Trouble walked arm-in-arm with her down the hallways and wherever she went. Coming behind her even ten years later was rough.

Althea often played hooky from school and frequently got sent home for fighting. The principal knew her name. He'd call mama and tell her that her daughter was being sent home for this or that. Then mama would meet Althea at the corner bus stop with a broom.

Sometimes, I would tell on Althea when she got in trouble, which, of course, only amped the heat in our already-steamy sibling relationship. We'd butt heads about anything when we were kids. It's interesting because, years later, after mama died, Althea and I became the closest of friends.

I was taught by the same elementary-school teachers Althea had.

A lot of them assumed I was going to be the twin of my sister. Consequently, I tried my best not to be the little trouble-maker that she was. Nonetheless, I did cause some problems. I was spoiled and believed everything should go my way. For sure, I didn't want anyone telling me what I could or couldn't do.

I remember a third-grade teacher warning me to leave this little boy alone, but I had other plans. I don't remember what he did to me, I just knew he was going to pay. A friend and I locked him in the girls' bathroom. Everybody got a piece of me that day. I got whipped by the principal, the teacher, my mama, my uncles, and aunts. It was horrible. But it taught me a lesson I never forgot.

I started playing tennis in the fourth grade, and that helped my attitude a lot. Playing forced me to try harder in the classroom because John wouldn't let us on the court if our report cards were bad. You'd have to stay home until your grades improved. I was miserable whenever I missed a hot minute of tennis.

I was one of those students about whom the teacher would say, "You can do it if you want to, but you just want to do enough to get by." I could have been a much better student.

I don't know why, but mama decided to send me to Pershing Junior High (7th-9th grades), a mostly white school on the other side of town. It was a fifteen-minute bus ride and I totally hated it. I never missed an opportunity to tell mama how biased the teachers were.

Lori McNeil went there too, so that made it a bit more tolerable. Everything was separated along racial lines, and I couldn't understand why we were there. The white kids would eat at their tables, the black kids at theirs. The white kids sat on one side of the room; the black kids sat on the other side. Neither group ever tried to socialize with the other. For the most part, all the black kids who came from MacGregor stayed together and all the white kids stayed together.

Pershing teachers and administrators had a blame-it-on-the-black-kids mentality. In their eyes, we were the trouble-makers and rule-breakers. They never picked on the white kids, just us. White kids could be cheating during exams, but the teachers never caught them because they were too busy watching us. When a black student got a better grade than some white kids on an exam, the teachers assumed the black student cheated.

The teachers were never helpful. Through their eyes and body language, they sent endless negative vibes rolling toward black students. There were a few black teachers at Pershing, but they seemed more concerned about not being accused of favoring the black kids than they were about pointing out double standards. I guess it was kind of difficult for them, since the black kids were the ones most often sent to the principal's office.

I'm sure my continuous griping about Pershing helped convince mama to send me to the all-black Ross Sterling High instead of the mostly white high school. Clyde Drexler, a former NBA pro with the Houston Rockets, also attended Sterling. He was two years ahead of me. We met in Spanish class my freshman year. Sometimes, I would be so tired from practicing tennis and staying up late to do my homework, that I'd fall asleep in class. Clyde would wake me. He used to tell me that one day I was going to need to know how to speak Spanish. I would say that I'd learn it when that day came.

Then I'd lay my head back on my desk and cop some more Zs.

At the 1992 Olympics held in Barcelona, Spain, I was on the U.S. Tennis Team and Clyde was on the Dream Team. We hung out together a couple of times and tried to speak Spanish. We joked about how both of us should have paid closer attention in high-school Spanish.

Clyde looked out for me even when I didn't want him to. Like the time Cheryl Jones, Lori, and I bumped into him at a Magic Johnson party in Los Angeles. We thought we were *the* stuff, hanging out with the superstars. I had been told that the freaks came out of the bushes at these parties, but I didn't realize that the freaks were some of the prettiest people in the world. It blew my mind that these people would do anything to get close to superstar athletes. We had been there for about thirty minutes when Clyde took me aside and said,

"This is not a place for a champ, so you have to leave." He showed me to the door and watched me leave.

I was more than a bit peeved with Clyde for a while after that. We talked about it later, and he explained why I should never get caught in that kind of setting. He said that what's good for the guys is not always good for the ladies.

Sometimes he'd spend a long time on the phone telling me about some of the things women would do to get in bed with a player. To this day, I don't understand why a woman would stoop so low to be with a guy just for the night. Clyde encouraged me to respect myself first. If I were strong enough to do that, the man would respect me as well. He was right about that.

I feel so proud whenever I reflect that my childhood buddy, my homeboy, was named as one of the NBA's Fifty All-Time Greatest Players. Formerly a 6' 7" guard with the Houston Rockets, Clyde was once and probably still is among the top 25 all-time scorers. He is also among the top ten all-time best with a 20-plus career scoring average. He was on the Rockets 1995 Championship team and was named to the All-Star team ten times. He ended an impressive fifteen-year NBA career in 1998 to coach at the University of Houston before deciding, after two years of that, to resign, play a little golf and tennis, and spend more time with his family.

We've had a big brother/little sister relationship since high school. He never got a big head about his success and always kept his feet on the ground. I admire and respect him for being able to do that. I thank him today for looking out for me, and I thank him, too, for getting me all those good seats at the Rockets' home games.

My self-esteem was boosted a bit when I went to Sterling because teachers and school administrators treated their students with respect. We were disciplined and criticized when we acted inappropriately, but everything was done in a positive way. I was always told that I was just as good as the next person. The teachers didn't prejudge us or expect us to be trouble-makers just because we were black. My attitude about life started to change for the better in high school.

At Pershing Junior High, it was always a hassle for me to get excused to travel to play in tennis tournaments. Sometimes Lori and I submitted phony doctor's or dentist's appointments because we figured that was the only way that they would let us miss class. Taking risks like that back then cemented the friendship between us. Though we were the same age, Lori skipped a grade and was a year ahead of me in school. We saw each other mainly at tennis practice, went to movies together on weekends, and sometimes stayed overnight at each other's house. We didn't go to the same high school.

At Ross Sterling, everyone seemed excited and proud that I was doing so well in tennis. As long as I made up the work, they did everything they could to help me get the match-play experience I needed to become a better player.

I do have one really unpleasant memory of my high-school years. I flunked eleventh-grade English, and mama kept me out of tennis for a month. That was probably the most devastating thing that had ever happened to me in school, mainly because it kept me from trying to qualify for pro events, like the Avon Futures, which was held in the U.S. that winter. But mama wouldn't let me play anywhere until I brought my grade up. She felt that my education was more important than me playing in a tennis tournament. Flunking eleventh-grade English also earned me a seat in summer school.

It was disheartening to have to study during the summer while the other kids were at the park practicing. I couldn't go out there until after summer school each day. That was a rude awakening.

The most frustrating thing about it for me was knowing that I had gotten an 'A' in English the first semester. But that was with a different teacher. I don't think my second-semester English teacher, a young white lady, liked me.

On her first day in class she told the students that she had never taught "colored" kids before. That didn't go over well with me. So I raised my hand and said, "We're not colored."

She went on to tell this story about her first trip to Mississippi, where she saw two signs, one pointing to a "white rest room" and the other to a "colored rest room." She said she wanted to go into the one with the pretty colored wallpaper. I didn't think that was funny, and I let her know. Some people just don't get it.

I was ranked among the top juniors in the country during that time, and local newspapers often wanted to interview me. This teacher was always very critical of me and rarely wanted to help with the timing of the interviews.

Actually, a boyfriend of mine copied my answers on the English final and he got a B plus. He'd be out there, happily running track, while I flunked, so I was in summer school. That same teacher never let mama or the principal see my test. I guess my mouth was a bit too big, but I felt that I was telling the truth and she couldn't deal with it. I'm sure she was jealous because of what was going on in my life.

At that time in my life the only thing I cared about was tennis. I wasn't much of a reader. I was satisfied to do just enough work to keep me in John's program.

After mama kept me out of tennis for a month for flunking English, John kicked me out of the program for two weeks for fooling around. He noticed a bunch of passion marks on my neck after a bus trip from Princeton, New Jersey. Lori's brother, Eric, gave them to me. I was a teenager at the time and figured I was just doing what most teenagers were doing. Okay, I liked boys. No harm necking with someone you liked, as long as you didn't go too far. One of the older girls in the program had to drop out because she got pregnant. We knew something was wrong when she couldn't run the bayou and couldn't stay on the court very long. After that, the mother of one of my friends encouraged us to take birth control pills, just to be safe. We never did.

Larry Thomas and Sheldon Perry, two of the older players in John's program, made me promise them that I wouldn't have sex until I finished high school. They knew if I made the promise, I would keep it. I always kept a promise.

A year after I graduated, I lost my virginity to George Kennard, who also was in John's program. It had to be after school was over because I had promised that.

It's pretty interesting that George became my first lover. He was my best friend, someone I could talk to about anything; he was a pretty good tennis player as well. We'd stay on the court forever together, and John and the other pros really didn't mind. They actually approved of my relationship with George because we always came to practice. How could I be getting in trouble if I was always at the tennis court? They imagined I was under their control.

I was the kind of kid who thought things all the way through. George was someone who I knew I wouldn't look back at years later and regret the relationship. Now we're out of touch; he has a wife and children and a great job at AT&T, and I'm happy for him. He never really had a chance with me; first, there was my tennis—that always came ahead of any man. A couple of years passed; we drifted apart. Then there was Willard, and I ended up marrying him instead.

John knew he could keep me in check by threatening to keep me out of the program. When I got interested in boys, he and mama used to conspire a lot to keep me on the right track. He was like a father to all the kids, and we often went to him to talk about life and other things. We were young people inquisitive about the world. The one thing that is not good about John is that if you don't see things the way he sees them, you're wrong. There is no in-between with him.

Actually, John didn't have to really worry about me choosing a boy over tennis. Those two weeks of punishment I received for necking convinced me that I would never let a man or anyone else interfere with my long-range tennis plans. I decided that I would never be forced to miss John's program because of any boy.

During daylight, tennis was the only thing I truly wanted to do when I was a kid. My major distractions came at night. I just had to watch my favorite television shows: "The Flintstones," "The Jeffersons," "Gilligan's Island," and "Good Times." Of course, at that age, the girls thought the guy who played Michael in "Good Times" was cute, while the guys were watching for Thelma.

I liked Gilligan because he was so silly, and I liked to see Fred Flintstone get out of all those tight spots. I just had to watch anything with Jerry Lewis in it. I met him during the Thanksgiving Parade in Houston, the same year I got to the Wimbledon final. He was such a nut. I loved that voice and his body going every which way. I didn't miss any of the Jerry Lewis and Dean Martin movies.

I also used to like to go to the rodeos. When the rodeo was in town, it seemed like everybody in Houston dressed up in western outfits for the whole two weeks. They would start with bronco riding, and you might see some kids chasing pigs. Then they would have live entertainment. It's a big Texas thing. It's funny because when I mention the rodeo to people who are not from Texas, they say, "What?"

I saw the Jackson Five at a rodeo. Mama wasn't going to get us tickets for that show, but we plotted and decided to have my niece fake an asthma attack and it worked. Mama got us tickets. They let my niece have or do anything she wanted whenever she started crying and wheezing.

I never used drugs or got involved with kids who were using drugs when I was growing up. I think I once got a contact high at a Rick James concert, but I've never smoked. I was too scared to do anything like that.

Because I grew up in a mostly black neighborhood, I look at what's happening with drugs in our society quite differently from some of the players I met in the tennis world who come from wealthy white communities. A lot of people I knew and grew up with were drug addicts or had problems with drugs. I've seen addicts in the park where I learned to play tennis or hanging out on the corners of the streets in my community. It's really sad.

I'm convinced that unemployment and welfare are two of the main reasons why black people turn to drugs. It seems like when one generation is tormented by drugs, the next generation isn't hurt quite as much. That's probably because when you see an older brother or someone close to him die of an overdose, you realize that dabbling in highs is risky business. There's always going to be a generation that has problems with drugs; then the next generation avoids making the same mistakes. It goes in cycles.

I can't imagine an athlete using drugs, but many do. Former NFL pro Dexter Manley and numerous other well-paid pro athletes allowed drugs to mar their careers. I can't imagine how anyone can use a substance that he or she knows can be harmful. I guess athletes who use drugs must think they're invincible and that nothing bad will ever happen to them.

I should say that I know Dexter, and he's a wonderful person— proof enough that anyone, however nice, however well-intentioned, can get caught up in the drug system.

One thing I know for sure: drugs aren't coming from our neighborhoods. Most are brought in from other countries. Could the government stop the flow of drugs into our country? Sure it could. Does it really want to stop it? You tell me.

No one in the government wants to stop it because too much money is being made, and drugs keep poor people down and out. Until minorities wake up and understand what is really happening, we are always going to have problems with drugs.

Actually, I almost got busted for drug smuggling when I was a kid. Just joking! Here's what happened. We once rented a van to go to Detroit for a family reunion. My aunt gave mama a lot of plants before we left. She had them with us when we took a bus trip to Canada before going back to Houston. A Canadian ranger got on the bus and asked mama what she had in the garbage bags. She told him they were plants, but she didn't know what kind. He looked us and the bags over for a while, but he never looked in the bags; then he moved on.

When we got back to Houston, mama was really excited about putting the plants in the backyard. Her boyfriend, Mr. Turk Foster, told her not to do that. They were poppy plants. He said that if we put those plants in the yard we would attract a lot of visitors who'd expect us to host a dope party. That was so funny to me because mama was a nervous wreck after that. It was probably one of the few times in mama's life that something other than her children was to blame for making her a nervous wreck.

When I was 12, I went through a stage in my life in which I didn't want to be seen in dresses. I guess that's when the tomboy in me took over. Jeans were quite popular then. If I wasn't playing tennis, that's all I would wear. Mama and my sister Clara stayed on me about that. "You're a young lady and you have to wear dresses," they kept saying. I changed my attitude about wearing dresses when I was about 15. That's when I discovered that the cute boys liked girls in dresses. After that, you couldn't keep me out of a dress.

During my tomboy phase John tried to get me to attend charm school, but I wasn't ready to go that far with the "girl" stuff. John used to go out with this model Carol Dickson, and she thought that Lori and I needed to improve our posture, walk with style, and dress fashionably. I think Lori attended charm school for a while, but I didn't.

Leola Figarow was my best friend in high school. We actually met in junior high but didn't really get to hang out together until we got to Ross Sterling. We had a very interesting relationship because Leola would fight everybody, and I would fight nobody. She became my protector, and nobody would mess with me because they knew Leola would fight 'em. Even though I played tennis and she didn't, we still hung out together. She was extremely smart and often would help me with my homework. On test days, every teacher we had in common would move her to the other side of the room away from me.

Once, she even helped me dump a boyfriend. I agreed to go to the prom with this guy but later got asked by someone I really liked. I was scared to tell the first guy I changed my mind about going with him, so Leola did it for me. She's always good at smoothing things over. She probably found a way to say it had something to do with my tennis obligations.

Yeah, I showed up at the prom with someone else, but as everyone who knows me well knows, I'm a finesser; I've always been able to finesse my way out of stuff.

I went to the prom with Jackie Williams, a track star. He was very nice and would always let me have my way. Granny thought he was too dark for me. I thought that was crazy because granny was just as dark as he was. We had so many different shades in our family anyway.

The dark-skinned/light-skinned thing is *definitely* a part of the black community. My sister Clara and brother Rodney are the only fair-skinned blacks in my family. My color is right on the cusp between dark and light brown. I always felt that some of my aunts were more partial to Clara and Rodney because of their light complexion. Light-skinned, long-haired girls back then were always considered cute or beautiful no matter how they actually looked. And light-skinned guys were thought to be the handsome dudes, even if they looked like Gilligan. You could have a truly beautiful, dark-skinned girl and people still would pick the light-skinned girl as the homecoming or beauty queen.

It's interesting now because most of the top black models are dark-skinned.

The color thing still seems to be a not-to-be-discussed, hush-hush issue in most black communities. Spike Lee talked about it in his movie *School Daze*. Remember in the end: the film goes into slow motion—Spike Lee's kind of thing—this guy's ringing the bell and saying, "We all have to come together."

With as many problems as we have to deal with, it's really stupid for us to be squabbling about the color of another person's skin. I get really upset when I realize that some blacks are more color-conscious than whites. Rodney King's famous quote was, and still is, truly appropriate for our time. I, too, wonder *why can't we all just get along?!*

Of course, he was talking about whites and blacks getting along, but it applies to everyone privileged to be alive here. Things get tough enough without fighting each other.

# 6

# Fortnight to Remember, Round 3

## *Garrison vs. Andrea Leand*

SOME TOP-RANKED PROS get downright indignant when they're not assigned to play on one of Wimbledon's show courts. I've watched several stars complain forever on their way to one of the outside courts.

Even though I was a top seed, I didn't feel insulted about playing my third-round match against Andrea Leand on Court No. 13, which is about fifty yards from Centre Court. I never cared where they put me.

And though I'm very superstitious—as you already know—playing on Court No. 13 didn't stir any concerns about bad bounces or bad luck. My first-round victory against Samantha Smith was played on Court No. 13, and that was a smooth, problem-free encounter. I mean, I was like, "Thirteen? Bring it on!"

Andrea and I had played against each other dozens of times in USTA junior events throughout the U.S.; she was a good friend and traveling companion when we were wet-behind-the-ears rookies on the pro tour. In January 1981, Andrea, who grew up in Baltimore, was the No. 1 junior in the nation. I was No. 2. We met frequently in the finals of national junior events and always played tense and highly competitive three-set battles. Her mother Barbara and father Paul, a surgeon, sometimes traveled with Andrea. They were always very nice to me. Andrea's grandfather, Herman Goldberg, also was especially kind and warm whenever he saw me. It never seemed to matter to them that Andrea and I were major rivals, vying for the number-one USA junior ranking. Who held the edge? Well, let me just say that at the end of 1980 she was number one in the nation (something I never actually achieved), but at the end of 1981, I was number one in the world and she was number two.

In our only previous meeting as pros, I beat Andrea 4–6, 6–2, 6–3 at the 1983 Virginia Slims of Houston. Though ranked in the top 50, Andrea left the tour in 1985 to attend college. She returned three years later with a degree in psychology from Princeton. Yeah, she's pretty heavy. Andrea quickly climbed high enough up the rankings ladder to gain direct entry into several major events, including the 1990 Wimbledon.

HBO televised parts of my match against Andrea. While on the air, former pro Billie Jean King, an HBO analyst, praised Andrea for having the courage and determination to return to the tour after such an extended absence. The break didn't seem to hurt Andrea's game that much. She beat Jennifer Santrock 6–3, 7–5 in the first round and Laura Garrone 5–7, 6–4, 7–5 in the second round, so I knew she couldn't be taken lightly.

Actually, I had hoped to engage in a little pre-match chit-chat with Andrea, just to learn how things were going on the comeback trail. When we were juniors, we yakked about clothes, dating boys, everything except tennis. Now that we're retired and single, we still yak about clothes, dating men, everything but tennis.

We didn't see much of each other at Wimbledon, though, mainly because of the All England Lawn Tennis & Croquet Club's locker-room caste system, something else that distinguishes Wimbledon from any other tennis event.

I was fortunate enough to be assigned to locker room A, which is used only by players ranked in the top 16. (Wimbledon seeds its own players, the only tournament to do so.) It's a spacious facility. In locker room A, the players' names are taped above their assigned stall. Each player is pampered and treated like members of the royal family. Top 10 pros get escort service, too. Just before my match was to start, members of a security force arrived in the locker room to escort me to Court No. 13. The paths to the outside courts are greatly congested, so security officials are needed to clear the way for the players and to keep fans from slowing the players down by asking for autographs.

Players ranked from No. 17 up to No. 128 and doubles use locker room B. Locker room C is for the rest of the players, who pretty much have to fend for themselves. That's where Andrea was. "It's much smaller," she told me, "and the players receive very little special treatment."

Believe it or not, Andrea didn't have a clean outfit to wear for our match that day. "Everything was dirty," she recalled. "I had just recently returned from school and didn't bring that much to wear. I really didn't think I'd make it this far, so I just ran out of clean clothes."

She borrowed a shirt from Pam Shriver and a skirt from Helen Kelesi. Andrea knew about my superstitious ways. Years later, she admitted that she had thought of trying to mess with my mind by reminding me not to step on any lines during the match. She decided not to say anything, and I doubt if anything she might have said would have made a difference anyway.

I pounced on her from the moment the match started and never let up. Leading 5–0, I closed out the first set with a flawless service game. I won the first point on a backhand volley, forced Andrea to push a backhand return into the net on the second point, slapped a forehand passing shot down-the-line on the third point, and crushed a forehand volley winner on set point. I broke Andrea's serve early in the second set, which was all I needed to be among sixteen players advancing to the fourth round. I defeated Andrea 6–0, 6–3.

The victory catapulted me into the second week of Wimbledon.

That's when the stakes get higher, the competition keener, and a player's will to win, not talent, invariably decides which player moves to the next round.

The second week also is when tennis fans get to learn a lot more about a player's personality through television exposure. Commentators relay more about our personalities and background during a match, and the viewers can make their own judgments about our mental toughness as well as our talent by watching how we play the key points. When the camera zooms in, viewers also get to see what we look like up close. In my early years, that was bad news for me because I routinely had bad hair days.

Sweat has never been good to most black women's hair, so there were times when the camera wasn't Zina-friendly. Lori didn't seem to sweat as much as I did, and it really used to bug me that she could look so cool and dry with her hair cut short. During the last few years of my career, I wore a cap to keep the sweat from streaming down my face. A lot of friends in Houston didn't know who I was without my cap. It seemed like I'd always have my worst hair days whenever I was interviewed immediately after a tough three-set match on a hot day.

Of course, if I were playing now, I would take more time with my appearance. These days image is everything. Unfortunately, it means more money, too.

Velma Nellum, who has been like a godmother to me for the past ten years, was the first person to make me aware of the need to take extra time to prepare myself before going on camera. She also scolded me when I didn't smile or look directly into the camera. I think tips like that helped me widen my fan base. I had begun to understand, too, that companies in search of top athletes to endorse their products expect the athletes to look their best at all times, particularly when cameras are rolling.

Velma and her husband Al live in Reston, Virginia. They're two of the most aristocratic black people I've ever known. Al is about 6' 2", dark-brown complexioned, has salt-and-pepper hair, and wears a beard. Now retired, Al headed A. L. Nellum & Associates, a management-consultant business based in Washington, D.C. Velma, a petite housewife with beautiful brown hair and such caring eyes, moves through life with enviable style and grace. She's the type of person you'd want to see in charge of a charm school for young girls.

John introduced me to them early in my career. They love tennis. I'd often spend time with them in Paris for the French Open and in London during Wimbledon.

Recalling those years, Velma said, "Zina and I talked about different things, like how she should look when she went on the court. We discussed neatness and the importance of good grooming in general. I encouraged her to look directly into the eyes of any person she spoke to, even if it was just to say hello."

The Nellums also reminded me to thank the Lord each day during Wimbledon '90.

"We would pray together before her matches and also afterwards at the house," Velma recalls. "At various times during her career, we prayed on the phone and we read the Bible together. I think spiritually, she has come a long, long way and has grown a lot."

Once in a while, I'd run into people who I could tell were looking for me to give them something. It was part of the world I grew up in. The Nellums weren't like that. Neither has ever asked me for anything, and both have given so much of themselves. Al, who had ventures in Europe and Africa, frequently talked to me about business from a global perspective.

Explaining their motivation, Al said, "We felt that young people like Zina who were out on the tour without sponsorship or camaraderie were vulnerable and needed guidance. Zina was shy and obviously in need of support. As she grew older, as our relationship grew, Zina moved naturally to have more contact with and dependence upon Velma as a woman. We kept in contact by phone when we couldn't be with her. For as long as I can remember, we always had her schedule and knew how to get in touch with her. She would call and say, 'I'm doing a show or event and here's the number where you can reach me.' That was before beepers and things like that became popular."

I was fortunate, too, to have met Motown's Berry Gordy a year or two before Wimbledon '90. John introduced me to Gordy, who was the force behind one of the music world's greatest assembly of superstar soloists and singing groups. Diana Ross, Michael Jackson, Smoky Robinson, and the Temptations started with Motown.

Gordy liked tennis and used to watch me play at tour stops in Los Angeles and San Diego. He asked me to participate in an image-enhancing experiment. His goal was to learn if the same image-enhancing techniques he used to increase the popularity and appeal of an entertainer could have a similar positive effect on a top athlete like me. He wanted to prove to me that it could be done.

He hired a lady named Bridget Hawn-Styles, a Los Angeles publicist, to work with me—or work on making me over is more like it. Bridget's job was to put together a press kit and get me more exposure, not just in sports publications. She contacted public-relations directors at *Ebony, Essence, Jet,* and some of the white glamour magazines as well. She did a really great marketing job.

Another assistant of Berry's recommended facials, which helped clear up blemishes on my skin. He explored whether I should change my hairstyle—get a cut or maybe a weave. He was trying to determine the best hairstyle for me to wear while competing.

We decided that I should wear my hair pulled back and rolled into a bun. I used hair pins to keep it tight and a head band to help keep the sweat from rolling down my face. That's the way I wore it when I played Andrea.

# 7

# Turning Pro

M Y FIRST NOTION of what it would take to become a tennis pro came in the summer of 1980. I was 16 when Althea Gibson invited me to her camp in Boston to practice with several black touring pros, including Leslie Allen, Kim Sands, Andrea Buchanan, and Renee Blount. They were getting ready for Wimbledon's main event. Practicing with the touring pros was an eye-opener. Doing it while under the watchful eye of Althea was my wildest dream come true.

Althea, a gifted serve-and-volleyer, was one of the game's top players in the late 1950s. People used to ask me if my sister Althea was named after the great tennis champion, but I don't think so. I would be very, very shocked if my mama had paid any attention to tennis when she was coming along.

Althea was the first black player to dominate the women's game at the highest level. I never saw her play, but people who did say that she could have won many more major titles. Unfortunately, she played when racial segregation was lawful and most whites didn't seem to want blacks to succeed in anything, regardless of how great or accomplished they might have been.

There was no prize or endorsement money in women's tennis in those days. Unable to make a living as a tennis player, Althea walked away from the game after winning her second consecutive U.S. Open in 1958. She sang professionally for a while and spent a few years on the Ladies' Professional Golf Association tour.

Althea worked our butts off for ten straight days at camp, but I never complained. I went to that camp because I was determined to show I belonged. As the youngest, I knew the unwritten rules. I couldn't quit or show any signs of weakness. If I did, I'd be dead meat.

We did mental drills, physical drills, and every other kind of drill. It became clear to me that playing at the pro level required much more than physical talent and preparation. Total concentration for extended periods of time was essential. Althea gave me a lot of one-on-one attention. She pushed me as if I were a pro, not a junior. She wouldn't let me be a wimp when being a wimp was all I wanted to be.

I was used to training on a tennis court from dawn to dusk, but not at that level of intensity. I learned to play one ball at a time, from point to point. Althea frequently stressed the importance of playing every point as if it were the match. That sounds easy, but it's tough to do. After hours and hours of working at my maximum mental intensity, I realized how far I was from where I needed to be. I think Althea's goal was to get me there in ten days. She told me time and time again that nothing was going to be given to me, and that I would always have to work harder than the white girls on the tour. She said I had to be far better than everyone else, and even then I'd probably find myself in a situation where being the best wasn't good enough.

Actually, Althea's training camp raised questions in my mind as to whether I was mature enough to make the necessary commitment. I learned during those grueling sessions that tennis—played at the highest level—was 90% mental. I wasn't sure I could develop the discipline needed to reach that level of consistency. For a while, I thought of giving up the game. I went home and actually quit tennis for a week. But it was too late; unknown to myself, I had already made a life commitment. I couldn't *not* play. This was the game I would grow to love.

When I resumed playing junior tournaments, I noticed how much stronger and more confident I had become and how smartly I played. I could really see the improvement. But I knew I'd need a lot more work before I'd be ready to challenge the world. So I started doing extra drills and roadwork — wind sprints and jogging.

In early 1982, I got a call from Tracy Austin's coach, Robert Lansdorf. He asked me if I wanted to practice with Tracy, who recently had captured the 1981 U.S. Open. Obviously, I didn't think twice about accepting his invitation. Tracy was the first pro I hit with who helped me realize what professional hitting at the highest level was really like. The intensity and velocity of her groundstrokes were greater than I was used to. She rarely hit short balls, made careless errors, or failed to put away an easy shot. Her shots were flat and nearly always landed on or near the baseline. Her approach to our practice sessions was business-like, with no room for "girl talk" or idle chatter. One session with Tracy helped me realize what Althea was trying to convey about working harder and striving for perfection on every shot. Though I was then ready to make the commitment, I still needed continuous exposure at the "Tracy Austin" level. That would require more money than the Garrisons could afford.

I was too young and immature to appreciate some of the sacrifices my family made during my junior years. I do now. We didn't have a lot of extra funds, but my family always managed to come up with enough to send me to play national and international junior events.

Mama, Lori's mom Dorothy, and their friends often held fish fries to raise money, and my sister Clara persuaded a night-club owner she was dating to let her sponsor teen dances on weekends to raise money. I also won scholarships and sportsmanship awards to finance my trips. Many times my family just passed the hat for donations.

Not too long ago, my brother Rodney told me that when I was

14 and played in the JAL Cup, a junior event held in Japan during Christmas, everyone decided that they would chip in and pay for my hotel instead of exchanging gifts.

"That was the first time as a family that we all realized that maybe some day our baby sister would be something," Rodney remembered. "Our big gift was waiting by the telephone that Christmas Day for a call from Zina. She didn't call right away because she figured we would hear what happened on the television. When she finally did, we were glad to hear from her. We never told her about what we had given up that Christmas."

Just being able to visit a foreign country like Japan was enough of a gift for me. I was told to be careful what I ate, so I didn't try very much. My diet in Japan consisted mainly of bread. I didn't like the taste of Japanese food then. Now Japanese and Chinese dishes are among my favorites.

Staying hungry physically must have kept me hungry as a player. I returned home that year with the JAL Cup championship, which was my first international title. Other than my gratitude and love, that was the only Christmas gift I brought home to share with my family.

John got help for my training from some of his business contacts. He didn't want me to have a lone sponsor because he didn't want anyone to come back in later years saying that I owed them something. If I had any doubts about turning pro, they disappeared during my senior year in high school when I won Wimbledon, U.S. Open, and the JAL Cup junior titles.

Would you believe I almost didn't get to play Wimbledon or the U.S. Open juniors? Even though I was ranked No. 2 in the country in the Girls 18-and-under and reached the French Open junior quarterfinals, I was the sixth person out to be chosen for the Wimbledon junior draw. That means that five other U.S. players got in ahead of me. And though I won Wimbledon, the USTA put me on an alternate list to get in the U.S. Open junior draw. That was the way the

USTA chose juniors back then, and John was really hot about it. The experience also reinforced what Althea repeatedly had warned: Even when you unquestionably have proven yourself to be the best player, you're not always going to be recognized as the best.

That was my first real brush with USTA racism at the highest level. That kind of thing still happens to blacks in the USTA across the board. It got in the way of Chanda Rubin when she was advancing. It bit MaliVai Washington, Lori McNeil, Katrina Adams, and every other black player. We were often pushed back from getting into an event, receiving an award, or just being properly recognized when it was obvious that recognition was deserved.

But I must give credit to the USTA for establishing one program that helped blacks develop as tennis players. Prior to 1968, the USTA reserved spots in the main U.S. Open draw for several top ATA players. A few years after the Open era began, the ATA national men's and women's champions were admitted directly into the U.S. Open qualifying event, not the main draw. I won the ATA title in 1979 and 1980 and made my U.S. Open debut in '80 as a qualifier. I don't remember how much first-round losers received back then, maybe a couple of thousand dollars. I couldn't accept money then because I was still an amateur. In 1997, first-round losers at the U.S. Open got about $10,000. I suspect the increase in prize money to first-round losers is one of the reasons that ATA champions no longer receive wild cards into the main draw. The ATA men's and women's champions now receive berths in the U.S. Open qualifying event. Though I rank the U.S. Open a notch below Wimbledon in my heart, it always will be a special place for me because it was the first Grand Slam tournament I ever played. Plus, after all, Wimbledon is viewed in England much as the Super Bowl is in the U.S.—the whole country gets involved, including non-tennis fans.

Lori qualified for her first U.S. Open by winning the 1981 ATA title. She beat me in the ATA final that year in the only match that I "tanked," which means I lost intentionally. John told me to lose, since I had already qualified for the U.S. Open as a result of being

83

selected to the U.S. Wightman Cup team. By tanking I helped make history. In 1981, two black women, for the first time ever, played in the U.S. Open. The fact that I tanked isn't something either Lori or I felt good about, but it shows what we were sometimes pushed to do for equal access.

Anyone who saw that ATA final between Lori and me knew something was fishy. I jumped ahead in the first set, then pretended that I hurt my leg. I started limping on one leg, forgot which leg I was supposed to have hurt, and started limping on the other leg. People realized what had happened and they were mad with John for making me do that. But John was absolutely right because I was already in the U.S. Open and Lori wouldn't get in unless she won the title. It made sense to me to try to have two black women competing at a Grand Slam event.

I wanted Lori to turn pro with me so we could be on the tour together, but she decided instead to go to Oklahoma State University. John wanted her to turn pro, too, but Lori stuck by her guns, insisting that she wasn't ready.

"I decided I had to take a different route to the pros," she recalled recently. "I pretty much elected to go to college because I knew my parents didn't have the funds for me to just travel around playing satellite events. By going to college I was able to get the school to pay for me to play in some of those events. Besides, I had seen all the top players like Chris Evert and Martina Navratilova, and I didn't think I could beat them. But after I got on the tour I found they weren't as tough as I had imagined."

After winning the world's major junior titles and being ranked the No. 1 junior in the world, it was pretty clear to me that I was ready for the pro tour. But mama and a couple of my sisters didn't think so. You wouldn't believe the bullshit we had over my decision to turn pro.

Mama, Clara, and Judy were on one side, saying I should go to college. John and I were on the other side, saying I was ready to be a tennis pro. It was a bitter battle.

Judy told mama not to let me play because girls shouldn't be sweating like that all the time. She thought it was unladylike to sweat. Clara thought John had too much influence over me.

I had spent most of my childhood learning about tennis and life from John. Naturally, I looked upon him as the father I never knew. And, naturally, some family members became jealous of John because of his influence over me. Whenever I made up my mind about anything, my sisters would say, "What does God have to say about that?" That's what they called John.

One day mama got tired of me talking back to her about turning pro and came to the park with this old rusty gun in her purse. She said, "I brought you into this world and I can take you out."

I said, "Mama, that gun is so rusty it could backfire on you." It was unusual for her to come to the park, and I knew I was going to get a whipping right there. Instead, I got a whipping when I got home. That's how frustrated she was with the whole situation.

I just kept saying, "Mama, I want to turn pro, I know I can do it." Coming from the old school, mama wanted so desperately for me to go to college. My thing was: I had beaten every top junior in the world, so I felt ready to move up to the next level.

She finally agreed with me. Soon afterwards, I held a press conference to announce the decision. I think everyone in my family was impressed with the media turnout and the fact that Arthur Ashe showed up as well.

I admired Arthur so much during my early junior years. I just couldn't believe that a black man was playing tennis at such a high level. You could actually see him on TV. All thirty of John's juniors watched Arthur beat Jimmy Connors in the 1975 Wimbledon final. We sat in that little tennis shop with our eyes glued to the set. When the match ended, we raced to the court. Everyone wanted to hit that slice backhand the way Arthur did against Connors. John always pointed out that Arthur not only played like a champion but carried himself like a champion. Nothing seemed to upset Arthur. I remember when we first met, he was very soft-spoken. Everybody loved him. On several occasions when I was a junior, Arthur came to Houston to help raise money for John's program. I know my decision to help other blacks get into tennis has been influenced by Arthur's example.

Life as a pro during my rookie year was no cup of tea, especially since I was out there by myself. I couldn't afford to pay John to travel with me, but I certainly needed him.

I missed my graduation so I could make the 1982 French Open my first tournament as a pro. I loved playing on clay. Yet I lost in the quarterfinals to Martina—the first of many to her. It wasn't a bad effort for a career debut. Afterwards I went back home to go to the prom. All my friends were excited about prom night, but I found the whole experience to be a bit dull compared to Paris.

Paris provided the only bright spot in a pretty dreary first year. Andrea Leand, my third-round opponent at the 1990 Wimbledon, also joined the pro tour in 1982. We traveled to Europe together that year and played doubles together at several events. We rarely won in doubles, probably because we were two teenagers impatient to be No. 1 in the world in singles.

It didn't take either of us long to notice that the level of competition was a lot tougher on the pro tour than it was in the juniors, and that our day-to-day existence as pros was dreadfully lonely compared to our junior years. We felt sorry for ourselves after we both lost first-round singles matches in Stuttgart, Germany. Recalling our effort at that event, Andrea remembers saying, "Oh God, is this what it's going to be like?"

Though I didn't have a world ranking, I was able to play the French Open and other tour events because I had won Wimbledon and U.S. Open junior titles the previous year and was considered a promising young pro. Tournament officials gave me a wild card, which meant I didn't have to play in the qualifying event. Nearly every pro event holds qualifying tournaments that give several low-ranked pros a chance to play in a major. Other low-ranked pros can gain direct entry at the discretion of the tournament director through the issuance of wild cards. Top teens and former top teens, including Jennifer Capriati, Martina Hingis, Anna Kournikova, and Venus and Serena Williams, routinely received wild cards before they became top stars. The major sports firms, IMG and Octagon, sometimes help their clients get wild cards into events that the firms manage. William Washington, father of former pro, MaliVai, frequently has criticized the USTA and officials at other pro events for not using wild cards to help low-ranked black pros.

I still look back at our family squabbles over me turning pro as one of the most depressing times in my life. I must have spent three months sitting in a corner trying to figure out what was going on and why people were fighting about whether I should go to college, not go to college, or play professional tennis or not play.

I probably would have gone to Southern Methodist University if I had decided to go to college. I knew Dennis Ralston, who was SMU's coach, and Rodney Harmon, one of SMU's top players. Rodney and I signed with the same agent, Bill Shelton. Later, I'll have more to say about Rodney and also about some of my more unpleasant experiences with agents.

The crux of my problem during that time was that I knew I would have to upset and disappoint mama in order to do what I thought was best for me. To this day, I believe if I had stayed as mean and selfish as I was then, I would have become No. 1 in the world. Over the years, I lost some of that fight, though I had enough to become No. 4. Mary Joe Fernandez and I have been told that we were too nice, that we had to be much meaner if we wanted to win a Grand Slam title. That has always bothered me. But in a way, you do have to be pretty darn selfish and single-minded to be a dominant tennis pro. I thank God that I turned out the way I am. You can always look back and say, 'What if I had been more like Steffi, more like Chris, more like Martina, or more like Monica.' That's a mind game I don't even care to play.

I don't think I need to cast doubt on my accomplishments by wondering what would have happened if I acted differently. I am who I am. I did what I did. No one can take that away from me. I was especially delighted to be me on the middle Sunday of the 1990 Wimbledon when I was among the sixteen players still in contention for the game's most coveted crown.

# 8

# Fortnight to Remember, Round 4

## *Garrison vs. Helena Sukova*

WITHOUT FAIL—and without really thinking about it—I got into my I-am-ready-to-get-my-groove-on mode whenever I reached the second week of a Grand Slam event. It's an ego thing. If you're a top seed, you expect to be still in the hunt during the second week. You live to feel the extra tenseness in your body and the tightness in your gut. And you know something's wrong if those usual symptoms of nervousness don't show up.

My second week at Wimbledon began with a fourth-round match against Helena Sukova of the Czech Republic. Helena, who is 6' 2", played a solid serve-and-volley game. Her wide wingspan made it difficult to get passing shots by her or to launch lobs over her. She had a wicked overhead, so short lobs were a definite no-no.

Helena beat the crap out of me the first four times we played, but I defeated her 6–3, 6–1 in the quarterfinals of a grass court event in Sydney, Australia. I beat her again (6–4, 6–1) two weeks before Wimbledon in the Dow Classic final, a grass court tournament in Birmingham, England.

Helena was tougher for me to play on a hard surface, but when

I faced her on a grass court, my quickness gave me an edge. She's slow and gangly and has trouble with her movement on a slippery surface. My game plan was to play aggressively and establish control of the net as quickly as possible. I did that by scrambling to the net behind nearly every one of my serves and by sneaking in on her second serve as often as possible.

Major upsets most often occur during the first week, when the top players' nerves are as skittish as the balls bouncing on Wimbledon's slick surface. Top-ranked players sometimes need a little luck to sneak through that first week.

Naturally, I felt really good when I began the second week with a no-sweat victory. I reached the Wimbledon quarterfinals for the third time in my career by defeating Helena 6–3, 6–3. My game was in sync, my mind was focused, and I was confident that I had a legitimate shot at going all the way.

My racket swing was sure and my contact with the ball was consistent. And I hit everything in the racket's sweet spot. I knew I could only get better. Sports agents love to hear that kind of talk.

I'm sure that nothing gets an agent's adrenaline flowing like the roar of a crowd responding to his client's brilliant shot-making. If he's in the stands at the time, the agent feels the crowd's enthusiasm. If he's watching on television, in his mind's eye he sees the marketing potential that his client's success might generate.

The agent is thrilled because he knows that people watching in the stands or on television can clearly see the kind of clothes, shoes, or sleeve patches his client is wearing. The agent knows he can use his client's extended exposure at a Grand Slam event to demand a heftier endorsement contract at renewal time.

Before Wimbledon '90, I had been ranked among the top twelve players in the world for seven consecutive years, but I had no major clothing or shoe deal.

Do I blame the absence of endorsements on race? To some degree, yes. But I also understand that it would have been more difficult for the major companies to ignore me if I were a Grand Slam champion. Black superstars receive the same endorsement opportunities as white superstars, but some segments of white America are slow or reluctant to give black stars the same respect and recognition that they do white stars on the same level.

When I first turned pro, I signed a three-year clothing deal with Pony for $125,000 and a racket deal with Wilson for $75,000, which wasn't very much compared to what some much lower-ranked white players received.

Shortly after I signed with Pony, I ran into my Houston homeboy Clyde Drexler, who had heard about the deal. Clyde said, "Hey, Zina, now that you've signed with Pony, I want you to get me a Pony bag!" We still laugh about that.

Pony didn't renew my contract. I was told that a Pony official let it be known that the company wanted to go with a blue-eyed blonde. That decision proved to be quite controversial. In its May 11, 1987, edition, *Sports Illustrated* had this to say about Pony declining to renew my contract:

"... Then there's the case of the world's two top black women tennis players, No. 7 ranked Zina Garrison and No. 12 Lori McNeil. It is rare for a woman in the top 15 not to have an endorsement contract with a clothing company, yet neither Garrison nor McNeil has one. Pony had Garrison under contract for a while, but chose not to renew the deal. John Wilkerson, who coaches Garrison and McNeil, told *Tennis Week* that Pony officials 'said Zina didn't project what they wanted. They said they were looking for a blonde, blue-eyed white girl.' Wilkerson concedes that because the tennis market is predominantly white, Pony may have valid economic reasons for such decisions, but he also says the companies could 'push' black players effectively if they tried. Pony officials say tight budgets, not race, caused them to cut their ties to Garrison. The company is spending its money on a Golden Girl concept featuring a white player, body-suit-clad Anne White, who is ranked No. 46 in the world."

I could also mention Helena Sukova.

Obviously, I was a much better player than either Anne White or Helena Sukova, so basically they were telling me that color, not talent, is what Pony wanted to promote. That didn't sit well with me. Once again I was reminded, in a very painful way, that I was a black person trying to make it in a white sport.

That's when I truly understood why Chris Evert was looked upon as America's most beloved female tennis pro. Chris was always portrayed as an untouchable, unbeatable, perfect goddess. That's the way she looked to me during my years playing in the juniors. I don't think I ever thought of her as just a person like me, until I first played her as a pro.

I must give her credit for being media-savvy. She knew how to use the media and she understood that an ugly image or attitude could be damaging, if not fatal, to a career. I've never seen an unfavorable Chris Evert story or photo. I was always irritated with pictures of me because the photographers seemed to get me with my legs going in opposite directions or my tongue hanging out.

I've never read an article about Chris losing a match because she choked or "tanked." Every Chris Evert story I've seen was written with a positive spin, a pro-Evert setup. Chris Evert not only was a bonafide champion, but throughout her career she was portrayed with girl-next-door charm, someone who seemed incapable of bad thoughts or deeds. That was her bottom-line image and that's what made her so marketable. Of course, being blonde and blue-eyed didn't hurt.

One of the tragedies of the modern sports era is that many rich and famous black athletes have lost all or huge portions of their wealth partly because they've lacked bottom-line business savvy. Some were forced to spend their later years as paupers. Joe Louis was just about broke before he left boxing. Far too many black millionaire superstars, including Kareem Abdul-Jabbar, suffered major losses through unwise investments.

Sad stories like Louis' and Abdul-Jabbar's occurred mainly because

African-American athletes, who largely are raised in families without strong educational backgrounds, don't know that much about the financial world. We have no one to tell us how to save our money, how to spend or invest it. Most white athletes don't have that problem. They have parents or other family members who are familiar with mutual funds and stock market investments.

In my playing days the top athletes—black and white—received most of their guidance in financial matters from mostly white sports firms. That is changing now. A new generation of black athletes and black agents is learning from an older generation's mistakes.

I got my first exposure to the business side of tennis through my first agent, Bill Shelton, an African-American who was then with ProServ. He came to Houston to recruit me while I was still in high school. In the beginning, I thought Bill would be an ally who understood me and would find a way to help. It didn't quite work out that way. Instead, he caused some friction between John and my family and provided my first glimpse of the seedy side of negotiations and agents. That experience led me to view some agents suspiciously, in a negative light. At times, I saw them all as piranhas, looking to make a killing at any cost. I felt that you basically had to sell your soul to the agents, and they only cared about you as long as you were winning. If you're not winning, it's like you're not even there. As soon as they see someone better, they move on.

I think Bill's job was to bring the most promising black players to ProServ. Arthur Ashe and Donald Dell, ProServ's founder and CEO, were close friends. Arthur was among ProServ's first clients and had a lot to do with Rodney and me joining ProServ.

Sara Fornaciari became my agent when Bill left ProServ to stay with then-rising teen star Andre Agassi, who joined IMG. I liked Sara because she was gung-ho about women's tennis. And she was very aggressive. If she felt something was good for me, she'd try to get me in it. Even after I left ProServ, she would continue to look out for me. Sara's a straight shooter. Since I've retired, she has hired me to be a commentator for the Oklahoma City event that she manages.

Her other clients included Pam Shriver and Tracy Austin.

Sara would let me know exactly what the number-ten-ranked player in the world should get, what number nine should get, and so on. Sara and IMG's vice-president Stephanie Tolleson, who represents Monica Seles, have proven that women can do the job just as effectively as any man. I'd like to see the major sports firms hire more women agents.

Once in a meeting with Sara and several of her ProServ colleagues, I was asked to okay a dollar figure for an endorsement proposal that I thought was too low, and I told them what I thought the number should be. Shortly after that I was walking across the street in New York, and this colleague of Sara's came running from the other side of the block to jack me up. "Who do you think you are," he yelled, "Michael Jordan? How dare you ask for that kind of money?"

I felt that if I didn't ask for it, how would I know I couldn't get it? It doesn't hurt to ask. Plus, I wasn't asking for MJ money, just ZG money.

That experience made me question whether I could trust ProServ to negotiate in my best interest. I told John about it and that's when we decided to leave ProServ.

I also thought it was strange that I never had a social meeting with ProServ's top man, Dell. At the time, I was among his highest-ranked athletes. Maybe it was because of conflicting traveling schedules. Maybe it was just an oversight. Or maybe it was because he had little interest in the women's tour.

Regardless, I thought it was odd that I had never been invited to his office, other than for final contract talks, which he didn't attend.

I didn't put up a fight when John suggested I leave ProServ to sign with Superstar Enterprises, a Washington, D.C.-based firm headed by Kent Amos, an African-American. At the time, Ron Brown, the Secretary of Commerce who died in a plane crash in 1996, was Amos' attorney. Brown negotiated the contracts and other legal dealings I had with Superstar Enterprises.

I was stunned when I read about the crash that killed Brown and so many others. When it happened, I felt that once again a very powerful African-American had died prematurely. I knew he had made significant contributions to our nation. Texas congressman Mickey Leland also died in a plane crash. To have two powerful black men perish tragically the same way seemed more than coincidental to me. I wondered, 'What did they know?' People say if you work in the government and you know too much, things can happen. Many blacks hold conspiracy theories about the assassinations of Martin Luther King and Malcolm X. I realize it's hard to believe, but it's also hard to put out of mind altogether.

Working with Amos was okay, but he wasn't able to open any doors to endorsements. That's when it began to sink in that the big three sports firms—IMG, ProServ, and Advantage International (now Octagon)—controlled the marketplace. If you weren't in that circle, major companies rarely talked to you.

Still, I wanted to give a black firm a chance. So we signed with The Oliver Group, a Houston-based firm headed by Andy Moran. I figured that since he was close to home, we could keep better track of what was happening with my money. Unfortunately, my trust in The Oliver Group was short-lived. After an audit, we learned that Andy kept $50,000 that was due me from an event in Tokyo. We sued him and won.

Andy claimed that $100,000 was missing when I came from Amos' firm, but I never found out what happened with that money. Actually, I doubt if any money was missing. I think saying money was missing was Andy's way of luring me away from Kent Amos. Like I said, my early exposure to agents was more negative than positive. But during that time, I let others take care of my finances.

I often read about players receiving signing bonuses or guarantees. I never got a guarantee or a signing bonus. It might have gone to somebody else and I didn't know about it. During that time, everything went through John or my sister Clara. I was just told what to sign and I wasn't supposed to ask any questions.

It bothered me too that though I am one of only a few major female sports figures in the country, I received just a couple of small endorsement deals with companies in my hometown. Houston is a big city, and it seems like somebody could have used me as a spokesperson, if nothing else. I had small deals with Whattaburger and Bland Cadillac in Houston, but other than that, nothing. I've never endorsed any products for a major Houston firm. Warren Moon, former Houston Oilers quarterback, was on everything when he was here. Other football and baseball players had good deals with the city, too. Maybe Houston just didn't want to take care of its women athletes.

However, I do think Houston has been very supportive of some of the things I've wanted to do there. It's like any other city: when you're doing well, everybody is behind you. When you're not doing well, no one's behind you.

Jackie Joyner-Kersee and I often talked about our encounters with corporate people who seemed perplexed about how to talk shop with successful black women athletes. Jackie got several endorsements late in her career but, based on her achievements, she should have been the most courted female athlete of her time. I could never understand why Mary Lou Retton got as much as she did for winning the all-around gymnastics title at the 1984 Olympic Games in Los Angeles.

My hostile attitude toward agents improved a few months before the '90 Wimbledon when Octagon's Phil de Piciotto assigned Patrick McGee to handle my business affairs. Patrick spent his teen years in Atlanta and later earned a political science degree at Kentucky, where he was a pretty good collegiate tennis player. He was named to the SEC's All-Conference team and nearly was named an All-American. He says a loss to Richey Reneberg in the NCAA Championships kept him from receiving that honor.

"When I realized I wasn't going to make it as a pro, I thought that being an agent would be pretty cool," Patrick said. He gained access to the agent world when his college coach, Kentucky's Dennis Emery, introduced him to Bill Shelton, my first agent. Before representing me, Patrick worked with several other young players, including Halle Cioffe, a former NCAA women's singles champion. I tease him about being the company's gopher before teaming up with me.

Patrick still represents me. He has been a wonderful agent, as well as a great friend. He has shared my joy during the good times and stood by me through some very rough patches.

He was thrilled when I reached the quarterfinals and was confident that my performance would help land that big, overdue endorsement deal that I patiently had been waiting for and deserved. The possibility of finally signing a major endorsement contract made me think of mama. I wanted so badly for her to be with me during my time of good fortune. She was always there for me when I needed her. I still have trouble accepting the fact that she is gone. I'm sure I always will.

# 9

# Losing Mama

'M NOT SURE if there was a connection, but mama's health took a turn for the worse soon after I joined the tour and started staying on the road week after week.

Mama took insulin every day but still ate a lot of foods she shouldn't have been eating, especially sweets. She wanted to enjoy life full-time and always talked about dying happy. She seemed happiest when she was eating cookies, candy, french fries, or anything else that was a no-no for a diabetic. Like former president Ronald Reagan, mama loved her jelly beans. It seemed like she had at least a bag-a-day habit.

If I hadn't become a tennis pro, I don't believe mama ever would have watched a tennis match in her life. She never really cared that much about tennis and never learned to keep score. But she was always the first person I'd call after a tough loss or a bad day on the practice court. I could count on her to lift my spirits, to remind me of better days or to reassure me in the way that only a mother can.

I called home nearly every day just to check on her. Sometimes, I actually had to bribe her to get her to undergo treatment she needed. An early milestone in my professional career occurred when I reached my first final—the U.S. Clay Court Championship. The best thing about that was I got some significant television exposure. Mama was in the hospital at the time, but one of her doctors told me that she knew I had been on television.

Mama was pretty sick for several months during my first year on tour, but she always bounced back, flashing an infectious I'm-gonna-be-okay smile. We used to tell her that she had nine lives.

Her diabetic condition wasn't the only reason I had so many sleep-less nights. During one of my road trips, mama had a heart attack. At one point, she had to undergo triple-bypass heart surgery. She didn't want to have it, so I resorted to bribery. I said, "Mama, if you do this, I'll buy you any kind of car you want."

Mama had always liked Cadillacs, so I picked out a candy-apple-red Cadillac for her. I'm actually joking. It wasn't my car. I was just driving it. I had an endorsement with Bland Cadillac. Rodney rolled mama's wheelchair to the window so she could look out and see the car.

Even though she was feeling better and was supposed to have gotten out of the hospital before I left for the U.S. Open, she kept saying, "I'm not getting out and I'm not going to see you again." I said, "Yeah, yeah, yeah," just to humor her because I thought she was hallucinating.

She spent most of her hospital stay in the intensive-care unit but later was moved to a different floor after she improved and seemed out of danger. A loved one's illness can frazzle the nerves of the clos-est family, and ours certainly was no exception. Oftentimes, the rel-ative who is rarely in town takes the heat. My brother Rodney got really angry with me once before when mama was hospitalized. That time, I was away playing in a tournament.

We were sitting on a bench in MacGregor Park and Rodney was scolding me for not coming home or going to the hospital to see mama. I said something smart and he slapped me. Rodney's a pretty big dude, about 6' 2". He gave me a good whack and it really hurt. I remember taking off and running the bayou, all two and a half miles from Calhoun to MacGregor. That's something I'd do when-ever I felt weighed down by stress or was aching inside. I'd just run until I couldn't run any more.

I never asked him why he felt the need to slap me, and he never apologized for doing it. Strange as it might seem, that's just the way we are. We never try to work through any conflicts or bad feelings we might have toward each other. We'll get mad with one another, then kind of go on and eventually get over it. In fact, the next year, Rodney was the main person encouraging me to go play in the 1983 U.S. Open while mama was back in the hospital.

John traveled with me all the time during my second year on tour. I earned enough in my rookie year to hire him as my full-time coach. I left for the U.S. Open thinking mama was going to be okay. Then I started getting troubling vibes about her once I reached New York. John and I stayed in a rented house in New Jersey during the U.S. Open, and I never really got comfortable being away from mama during that time. I just didn't feel right. I woke up about 3 o'clock one morning numb with fear, with sweat running down my back. I went to John's room, woke him up, and said, "My mother just died, I know it, I just know it."

John calmed me down, got me back to bed, and told me to wait a few hours, then call home to see how mama was doing. When I called, Clara told me that everything was okay with mama and there was no reason for me to come home. Her words didn't ring true to me, and I didn't sleep a wink the rest of the night.

I lost my match that day and flew to Houston the next day. Rodney took me to the hospital. When we got on the elevator, he pushed No. 2, which was the intensive-care floor. Mama's room had been on a different floor when I visited her before the Open, so I asked Rodney, "Why are we going to the intensive-care floor?"

He said that mama was in a coma and wasn't doing well. He said they didn't want to upset me while I was playing at the Open, so they lied. He also told me that mama's heart indeed had stopped beating for a while but that she soon was revived. That seemed to have occurred about the same time I woke John to tell him about my premonition.

Mama never really got to see me at my best as a pro. She was hospitalized when I reached my first final and was in a coma when I won my first pro event in Indianapolis. She was even sick when I became the first black woman since Althea to be ranked in the top ten. I didn't pick up a racket for a month while mama was in the hospital.

She looked like a little baby when I saw her the day I came home from the '83 U.S. Open. I think she knew I was there, and I'm sure I saw a tear roll down her face. But the doctors said it was a reflex action and that she wasn't able to recognize anyone in her condition.

The next morning, I answered the phone and before my sister could speak, I said, "I know, mama died."

She said, "How did you know?"

"I just felt it," I said.

Sure enough, mama had died minutes before the call. I was just 19 when she left, and felt way too young to face life without my role model, my best friend. I thought I'd never shake the pain I felt that day. I just kept telling myself that my mama wasn't gone, that she was on a long trip somewhere. The pain truly is a lot deeper and hurts a lot longer when you lose someone who loved you just for being you and not because of how much money you have or what you might have achieved.

Mama's death drew the rest of the family closer together. My brother became the father of the family, and the twins Judy and Julia became the backbone. Clara acted like she wanted to be my mother. I was surprised how close Althea and I became, mainly because we used to fight like cats and dogs when we were younger.

Althea, our entrepreneur, is very ambitious and believes there's nothing she can't do. She was mama's problem child in school. She went to summer school every year from grades 7 through 12. She got wiser as she got older and made all of us proud by getting a degree in child psychology from Texas Southern. She now works with mentally retarded people and also owns her own convenience store and hair salon.

I remember when I preferred to stay at the park and play tennis in any kind of weather instead of being at home. I know I was a handful for my sister most of the time. Reflecting on the many times she had to fetch me from MacGregor Park, oftentimes after dark, Althea said, "Sometimes I used to just leave her out there, but when I came home without her, mother always would make me double back to pick her up. Chasing after Zina often interfered with things I wanted to do. I was the one who always had to pick her up. They used to get mad with me because I used to say, 'Why does everything have to be for her?' But it did pay off."

Like my father, Rodney is a postal worker. He's a pretty good athlete and probably would make a great baseball, basketball, or football scout. He can watch a kid perform in an athletic arena at the junior-high level and pick him to be a great athlete in college. He is right most of the time.

Rodney joined the Army when I was ten. He took that big step shortly after linking me to tennis through John. It tickles me when he talks about how much I had improved when he came home from the Army two years later.

"I had to cheat to get one game when I came back," Rodney said. "She was about twelve then and really had improved. I never really told her this, but when she was small her main question to me every day was: 'Can I make some money playing tennis?' The only thing my mother knew about tennis was that if you were a good player, you could go to Wimbledon. So Zina kept asking if she could go to Wimbledon."

Rodney also finished Texas Southern. Sometimes I believe he thinks that had he pushed me just a bit more, maybe I could have been No. 1 in the world.

As for Clara, oh Lord, I don't know how to describe her. In my early years on the tour, she was the one who traveled with me and kind of ran around trying to be my mother. Actually, she was quite helpful, especially as my fashion adviser. She taught me how to buy clothes and how to dress. We love her to death, even though she always finds a way to get what she wants. She's the spoiled one in the family. And smart as a whip. Alexis is her nickname. We called her that because she looked like and acted like Alexis Carrington of that TV show, "Dynasty."

Generally, my family has been very supportive and caring, but our family life hasn't been friction-free. We've had our share of conflicts and bad times. Even though everyone had jobs, there were times when I felt like I was the family's private ATM. They only came to me when they truly needed something, but it seemed like somebody needed something all the time. Rodney asked every once in a while, but he'd always pay me back. If either of the twins asked for something, I knew they really needed it.

They must have figured that having a rich little sister meant that they were rich, too. But I was never phenomenally rich, and I'm certainly not rich now. I remain deathly afraid of becoming that stereotype of the wealthy athlete, someone who neither knows nor cares about what happens to his or her money. That was never me.

My first car was a little bitty Subaru. My second was a 1972 Volkswagen. I was earning several hundred thousand dollars a year at the time, and many of my friends thought I was absolutely crazy for buying the Bug. Rodney found that car and restored it for me. My sister Althea burnt the engine out. I'm still mad about that. I also bought a townhouse after mama died. Clara and her husband lived with me for a while. Later I asked a girlfriend, Kim Davis, to stay with me. Coming from a big family, I never wanted to stay by myself.

I felt kind of guilty when I got my first Porsche, mainly because I didn't think I was earning enough money to afford it. I bought it when I was 22. I've since owned three.

As I got older, I grew strong enough to say "no" when family members made unreasonable requests. I told them they have jobs and I have a job. I let them know that I should be allowed to enjoy the things I have without being made to feel that I had to buy something new for everyone else. If there was a crisis, I'd help. Otherwise, I couldn't be a constant benefactor; I had to look out for my best interest and take care of myself first.

I doubt if white families go through as many changes when a family member comes into a lot of money. Most black folks from disadvantaged backgrounds just aren't used to having money. When a black athlete with six or seven brothers and sisters signs his first big contract, he becomes everyone's savior. I've known some family members to quit work, deciding that they can live off their rich relative. Athletes in that kind of situation usually end up broke in just a few years. Now that I'm retired, I really have to stick to a budget, like most folks on fixed incomes.

The most stressful times for me always occurred when a tour event was played in Houston. Everybody in my family, and I'm talking about more than sixty people, expected a free ticket to the event. On the day I was trying to get ready for a match, John told me that one of my relatives was demanding that I give them fifty-five tickets so everybody could see me play. The arguments over free tickets for family members often were brutal.

My sister Judy was good about making the others see how unfair and unreasonable they were. She told them that I was as much a celebrity as singer Luther Vandross, and that if they were willing to pay $25 to see Luther Vandross perform, they ought to be willing to pay as much or more to see me play. They didn't see it that way, though. I never could get enough tickets for my family and everybody else in the neighborhood. Still, everyone expected a free ticket. No one stopped to consider the absurdity of the request or the pressure I felt to please them while trying to prepare to do my job: play a tennis match.

Sometimes I would get so keyed up and emotionally drained by their demands that I'd get physically ill. I once played Gigi Fernandez in Houston and had to be taken to the hospital afterwards and treated for dehydration. Some members of my family were spaced out when that happened. Judy was crying, and Clara was worried that my toes looked bad because I didn't have any nail polish on them.

The doctors kept me overnight and had to pump a lot of fluids into me. When they checked my blood, they couldn't believe that I had no magnesium, no calcium, no potassium. I hated playing in Houston, and I never won a title there. Only once did I get to the finals, but I lost to Monica Seles.

I wonder how mama would feel about what I'm doing now that tennis no longer rules my life. I think about her every day. I miss the times when she took us fishing and crabbing in Galveston, which is about forty-five minutes from Houston. She would borrow a friend's truck and we'd leave at 4 o'clock in the morning.

We'd walk on the beach while the crabs were still on the banks. We'd scoop them up. I used to like to kick them with my bare feet and watch them rattle and scatter about. Mama warned me to leave those crabs alone. She knew I'd be bitten one day, but I didn't pay her any mind until one of 'em got me. I have two permanent marks on my feet to prove it.

Granny died two and a half years after mama passed away. I watched Granny gradually give up on life after mama died. I was playing a tournament in Brazil when I learned she had passed. I played a match shortly after I was told and couldn't keep one ball in the court. The flight from Brazil was dreadful, mainly because I just couldn't stop crying.

Granny was pretty special. She taught me how to cook, how to clean, and a lot about discipline. I can still see myself trotting outside to choose the switches Granny would use to whip my butt. I still think about Granny every time I see reruns of "The Beverly Hill-billies."

When mama died, I didn't really want to play tennis anymore. I didn't want to do anything. I lost fifteen pounds and constantly felt depressed and more alone than ever in my life. I was especially dependent on her. She packed my bags for every trip I took until I was 18.

I miss the talks we had about anything and everything. When I was a little kid, she used to tell me that whatever I decided to do with my life, I should always strive to be the best, even if I chose to be a housekeeper.

I was a stubborn little thing and rarely obeyed anyone, including mama. Once when I tried to lift a box that was bigger than I was, mama said, "Zina, you can't do that!"

I said, "Why not?"

Of course, I grabbed the box anyway, and when me and that box tumbled to the floor, I knew why I should have listened to mama's advice. Still, I tried to lift that "box" many times. I was a trial-and-error kind of child, a trial-and-error teenager, and a trial-and-error adult too. I learned what I shouldn't do by doing it. Obviously, that's not always the best way to get an education. But once I get it, you never have to tell me again.

Mama rarely let my stubbornness upset her. I was her baby, the last of seven children. She made me feel very special, like a queen. Sometimes I indeed imagined I was better than everyone else, especially my brother and sisters. When I wanted something and didn't get it right away, I'd scream bloody murder. Yeah, I was a big crybaby. But mama never tried to interrupt my crying spells. She believed that crying was a reflection of strength, a building block to good character, not a sign of weakness. Whether I was hurting emotionally or physically, mama encouraged me to wail away.

"Get it all out," she would say. "Learn from the experience and move on. Time eases all pain."

Mama taught me the most important lessons in life by her example, just by being herself. She encouraged me to trust in the teachings of Jesus Christ, to help others as I moved along life's highway, and always to treat others as I would want them to treat me. Mama didn't smoke or drink, and I don't believe she had a mean bone in her body.

I will forever cherish our time together, and I'll always regret not having done all the things we dreamed of sharing. I still shudder when I think about the many times I intended to go home to see her but couldn't. I wanted to be able to care for her as she had cared for me. But more than anything, I wanted her to hear me say, "Thanks for being there when I needed you, mama."

After she died, thoughts of mama frequently flew through my mind, especially on the eve of a tough match. I hoped mama would be there for me at the '90 Wimbledon when I faced Monica Seles in the quarterfinals. I believe she was.

# 10

# Fortnight to Remember, Quarterfinals

## Garrison vs. Monica Seles

ONICA SELES WAS RANKED NO. 2 in the world and was on a thirty-six-match winning streak when we clashed in the '90 Wimbledon quarterfinals.

She arrived at Wimbledon that year gunning for her seventh consecutive title. The giggly girl from Yugoslavia beat everyone in sight at the Lipton, U.S. Hardcourts, Eckert Open, Italian Open, Lufthansa Cup, and French Open. Then-top-ranked Steffi Graf succumbed to the left-hander's withering groundstrokes in the French Open final and in the Lufthansa Cup final, which was played in Berlin, Germany, Steffi's home turf.

A phenom at 15, Monica came out of the blocks in a sprint. She knocked off veterans Larisa Savchenko, Robin White, and Manuela Maleeva, reaching the semifinals in her pro debut at a Washington, D.C., event. Monica struck the ball with unexpected ferocity and played with the savvy of a seasoned pro.

Hey, I was there and I was really impressed. She twisted her ankle against Maleeva and decided to default about a half hour before she was to meet her next opponent: me.

Monica was 12 when she and her family left Novi Sad, Yugoslavia, to settle in Sarasota, Florida. She said and did a lot of kooky things during her early years on tour and surely plucked my last nerve more than once.

She told reporters that she admired singer/actress Madonna. At times, she acted as if she were the Madonna of the tennis world. She seemed to enjoy being a major topic in tabloid newspapers. Make that any newspaper.

I think of Monica as a person who brought a lot to the game when it needed a spark. But in her early years, I also saw her as an athlete whose major goal was to be an entertainer or a movie star, not a true champion. I don't know her that well as a person, but I know I've never been as angry at a player as I was with her when we met in the 1989 French Open third round. I had a serious problem when she tried that show business stuff by offering me a bouquet of flowers before our Center Court match at Roland Garros Stadium. In her book, *Monica: From Fear to Victory,* Monica said that some young girls at courtside gave her the flowers, but I remember Nick Bollettieri, who was then Seles' coach, handing her flowers to give to the crowd. She couldn't have realized how angry and insulted I was when she did that.

I wanted to jump across the net, take some of those flowers, and smash them in her face. I could almost see myself sticking the rest of them in Nick Bollettieri's face. Lord, forgive me for having wanted to do such dastardly deeds. And thank you for helping me maintain my composure then, and to understand now, that Monica knew not what she had done.

I remember standing on the court thinking that this girl has no clue what these people have gotten her to do. I felt she was being exploited. They were willing to do anything to try to get the public to like her. Never in my life had I felt that much rage. I lost that French Open match to her 6–3, 6–2, and all I could think about was those flowers and how furious I was.

Later, she did something else I didn't like. She told trainer Bob

Kersee, who was working with both of us, that if he was going to be her trainer, she didn't want him to work with anybody else in the top 20. I knew that Bob had been working with her because his wife, Olympic great Jackie Joyner-Kersee, told me that they had been with Monica in Sarasota. I thought that the people around Monica were telling her what she should be doing; she wasn't doing enough thinking for herself.

I'm sure the flower incident at the French Open was in the back of my mind when we met in the '90 Wimbledon quarterfinals. I was definitely psyched. Every time I thought about it, I wanted to break her streak so badly I didn't know what to do. But I knew, too, that I was going to have a battle on my hands.

Monica is one of the toughest competitors on tour. She goes for the big shot nearly every time and from either side, backhand or forehand. Yet for some reason, I was never afraid to play her. I felt I had the speed to run down her balls, regardless of the angle she hit or how hard she smacked them.

Our match was played on the old Court No. 1, which had a seating capacity of 6,500. Court 1 was adjacent to the much larger Centre Court (12,500). The place was packed, and everyone seemed a little surprised when I got off to a good start. I won the first set, 6–3; she bounced back to take the second set, 6–3. The final set was the most intense set I'd ever played.

My intensity level used to rise automatically whenever I played a Grand Slam event, especially Wimbledon. Maybe seeing Monica, the hottest player on tour, on the other side of the net gave me an extra surge of adrenaline. Though the roars from the crowd were at times deafening, I could hear clearly this voice inside my head telling me to stay calm, keep your eye on the ball and keep it flowing. And that's what I did. *"Ain't no need to worry what the night is going to bring/It'll all be over in the morning."*

I got two quick service breaks and jumped out to a 4–1 lead. I was "in the zone," which means I was playing with an eerie feeling of invincibility. It didn't matter how hard Monica hit the ball, I knew

I'd get it back. It didn't matter how well she angled the ball while serving or hitting groundstrokes into the corner, I knew I'd track it down.

I felt a oneness with the ball, like it was a part of me.

I learned later that in her analysis for HBO, Billie Jean King wondered aloud "if Zina can close the match out now that she's up?" I must have wondered the same thing at about the same time. One thing I knew for sure: Monica wasn't the kind of player who'd get behind, then roll over and quit.

It's tough to stay "in the zone" for an entire match. Sure enough, my seeming touch of invincibility disappeared for a while and Monica climbed back into the match. She broke me in the sixth game, crunching a backhand volley on break point, then held her own serve in the next game when I smacked a forehand long on game point. Monica broke me again in the eighth game with a backhand crosscourt winner.

Just like that, she had rallied to tie the score at 4–4. She might have thought that I was about ready to pack it in, but I wasn't. I slapped a forehand down-the-line winner to get a break point on her serve and afterwards screamed, "Yes! Yes! Yes!"

Then I lost my serve in the next game, making three consecutive errors: a forehand that landed a foot wide, a crosscourt backhand that was inches wide, and a crosscourt forehand that was inches long. In the next few games the momentum ricocheted from her side to mine, and back again. Leading 7–6 in the final set, Monica held a match point, but I shut the door on that opportunity with a screaming forehand winner, the kind I usually miss in big matches. I finally got my first match point in the 16th game. It was the only one I needed. I led 8–7 when Monica hit a mediocre shot that landed in the middle of the court. I crouched into position on my forehand side and nailed it for a down-the-line winner. I managed to breathe normally again only after I saw the final set score of 9–7 posted on the scoreboard. I won 6–3, 3–6, 9–7. Whew, what a match!

It was interesting for me to see how in her book, Monica talked about my forehand winner on the match point she held. She noted that I frequently had missed that shot on key points in other matches. I've got to give her credit for doing her homework on me because she was right.

That shot had plagued me the whole year. It was a short forehand in the middle of the court, which is basically what we would call a setup. It's not one that you're ever supposed to miss. It's like someone just feeding you balls with the perfect placement. Yet I would tense up and get so nervous that my arm wouldn't even move.

I had lost at least four previous matches by missing that exact shot—against Steffi, Martina, Conchita Martinez. I still think about the one I missed against Mary Joe Fernandez in the 1990 Australian Open quarterfinals. Every time I'd try to go down the line with that shot, I missed by inches. It actually started to bother me. I sought help from a therapist—Richard Austin—because I had this thing in my mind about not being able to hit a short forehand.

Most of the top pros have, at one time or another, used psychologists and/or therapists to help exorcise emotional demons or to find and fix imagined and/or actual flaws in their games.

Through therapy, I learned how to be calm when I got in that particular situation. It certainly paid off against Monica. Going for that shot, I felt at ease, at peace. Right before her match point, I remember falling on the court and being angry with myself. Then I relaxed, took a deep breath, and felt like my body was just floating. When I got that forehand on her match point, I just hit it. After that, I knew that I was going to win the match.

Monica isn't the same person she was then, so I don't look back at that victory with the same degree of glee I felt when the match ended. I believe Monica became more mature after she split with Nick Bollettieri. Having to deal with traumatic experiences at such a young age tends to expedite the maturation process. Tragedy already has knocked twice at Monica's door.

ZINA: MY LIFE IN WOMEN'S TENNIS

In April of 1993, Gunther Parche, a deranged Steffi Graf fan, stuck a knife in Monica's back while she sat in a courtside chair at an event in Hamburg, Germany. Her physical wounds healed within a few months, but the incident left a deeper emotional scar and drove her from the game for more than two and a half years. A few years later, her daddy died.

Monica showed a great deal of courage and strength then. She won a large bushel of admiration points from her fellow pros and fans because of the way she dealt with the loss of her father just a couple of weeks before the 1998 French Open. Understandably heartbroken, Monica considered not playing in the '98 Open. I was among those who were glad she changed her mind. Monica lost to Arantxa Sanchez Vicario in the final, but left Roland Garros a winner anyway. Her demeanor and effort under the circumstances were remarkable and truly inspirational. A warm and friendly man, Karolj was Monica's father, coach, confidante, and best friend.

I wish Monica much success, and I'll be rooting for her to do well during the rest of her career. I pray that she'll find peace of mind and happiness.

After upsetting Monica, a feeling of invincibility seeped into my bones. I didn't believe I could lose in any event, and up to that point, I was still in contention for not one but three Wimbledon titles: singles, doubles, and mixed doubles. Patty Fendick and I beat Jill Hetherington and Robin White 6–1, 6–7, 6–1 to advance to the women's doubles semifinals, and Ricky Leach and I beat Danie Visser and Rosalyn Fairbank-Nideffer 2–6, 6–4, 7–5 to gain a semifinal berth in the mixed doubles.

Everything was moving in the right direction for me during that time. I couldn't help but think about my family back home and the many friends and strangers who helped make that moment, that opportunity, possible. Despite all the early heartaches, disappointments, and days full of doubts, turmoil, and discontent, somehow I knew I'd eventually find the proper blend of people and purpose that would lead me to better and brighter days. My spirits were high, my faith was strong, and I felt good and truly believed I was on course to find happiness and success.

I felt, too, that all those potholes in the road that I encountered during my early years as a pro, damaging and disruptive though they might have been, helped make this part of the ride more balanced and real.

© Michael Baz

# 11

# Black Musketeers

Because I couldn't afford to pay him, John wasn't on tour with me during my rookie year. He joined me the second year mainly because I realized I couldn't afford to be out there without him. Coaches do make a difference.

Lennart Bergelin, a pro coaching pioneer, was Bjørn Borg's mentor/travel companion when the quiet Swede won six French Open titles and five consecutive Wimbledon crowns in the 1970s. By the mid-1980s, nearly all the top-ranked pros were traveling with full-time coaches. The really good coaches wear several hats. They often act as advisor, companion, confidante, travel secretary, as well as strategist and scout. Generally, coaches with players ranked in the top 10 make more than $100,000 per year. Those linked with superstars make even bigger bucks. Brad Gilbert probably made more than $1 million—including bonuses—in 1999 when his guy, Andre Agassi, completed a remarkable comeback. Agassi, who fell to No. 141 in 1997, captured two major titles—French Open and U.S. Open —and ended the millennium ranked No. 1 in the world.

The financial arrangement between a coach and a player earning more than $500,000 a year ranges from $1,000 to $5,000 a week, plus expenses, for twenty weeks per year. To most players, a good coach is worth every penny.

You need someone to arrange your practice schedule, point out your weaknesses, enhance your strengths, applaud your victories, share your joy, and help you through the tough times when your game just isn't there. You need a shoulder to cry on when you can't stop the tears. I know I did.

I looked upon John Wilkerson not just as a coach, but as a father figure. Nearly everything that needed to be done, I counted on him to do. He worked without payment during my junior years, but I paid him well while we were together on the pro tour.

Though I traveled alone during my rookie year, I was guided by John's playing philosophy and pretty much followed his directions off the court as well. John didn't want me to associate with other players and, for the most part, I didn't. He said he didn't want anybody to get to know me because he thought that might affect the way I would play against that person in a match.

When I won Wimbledon and U.S. Open junior titles in 1981, I worked out regularly with fellow black pros Andrea Buchanan and Kim Sands. I'd gotten to know them at Althea's camp a few years earlier. Though we came from different cities—I was from Houston, Kim was from Miami, and Andrea grew up in Compton, California—each of us had similar aggressive styles. We played all-court games. In fact, every black player on tour knew how to play the net.

Kim won the ATA women's title in 1976, turned pro in 1978. She reached a career high No. 46 in singles and No. 29 in doubles. Kim used to help by just discussing the different styles used by pros she'd played. She'd advise me on tactics and strategy.

"By example, we showed her that we weren't afraid to be out there," Kim noted recently. "I think the confidence we conveyed was very helpful to her. I don't think she sensed any kind of difference with us and the other girls, but she could identify with us because we were women of color. Zina smiled a lot; she was down to earth and a very good player. She beat all of us."

In January of 1982, the *Los Angeles Times* reported that Andrea Buchanan and a man were shot to death at an eatery. Andrea was 26 when she died. Kim left the tour for a while shortly after Andrea's death. They were very close friends.

"I had never known any young person to die," Kim said. "It was just shocking to me."

My life on tour became a bit more enjoyable when my childhood friend Lori left Oklahoma State in her sophomore year to turn pro. Finally, Lori, John, and I were back together again! Lori and I were as close as sisters with John as our coach and dad-on-the-road. Having two rising pros proved to be too much of a handful for John, so he asked Willis to share the load.

I first met Willis at the 1975 ATA Nationals in San Diego. He was there with eighteen juniors from his D.C. program; I was there with a similar-size group from John's program in Houston. Actually, we met Willis' kids before we met him. They flew to San Diego, but Willis drove. Later Willis told me that it was the first plane ride for his kids and that he used the money he saved by driving to take the kids to restaurants instead of fast food joints. John and Willis frequently did stuff like that for us, but we were too busy being brats to appreciate it at the time.

I think John was really impressed with the way Willis' juniors conducted themselves in San Diego before Willis arrived. They punched in for practice as if they were on time clocks. They were on the courts an hour before we were each day, stretching and exercising before running through a series of drills.

I believe John had that scene of Willis' well-disciplined kids in mind when he asked Willis to help him coach Lori and me. Willis had grabbed a few headlines by coaching Rodney Harmon, then the tour's top black male player, to a quarterfinal berth at the 1982 U.S. Open. Rodney was a rising star a bit before Lori and I made our move.

Rodney attended SMU during the school year but trained in Houston each summer. He used to run the bayou with us. I think he was pretty shocked when I finished ahead of him a few times. We played mixed doubles together at several events.

Reflecting on our training days together in Houston, Rodney moaned, "We used to run that bayou in the morning, practice for five hours, and then run it again in the late afternoon. After you ran it once, the last thing you wanted to do was hit a tennis ball. But the running never seemed to bother Zina. The pace was always quick, and she was the fastest female I'd ever seen. She never lost a match because she was out of shape. When she was at her peak, Zina always had an extra reservoir of energy that I'm sure she got from running the bayou."

He thought about that and added: "She's really tough; that's what I've always liked about her. Once when we played a mixed doubles match against Andrea Leand and John Newcombe, Newcombe hit Zina on the leg with an overhead smash. She just looked away and kept playing. Later, she smacked a forehand volley into his crotch. A few games later, I had a chance to hit Andrea with an overhead but pulled back and placed it away from her. Zina pulled me to the side and said, 'When you get an overhead, you've got to knock her out because every time they get the chance they're going to knock me out.'"

Rodney grew up in Richmond, Virginia, Arthur Ashe's home town. He got his degree from SMU, played on the tour until 1986, then gave it up because of injuries. He worked as a USTA junior coach, spent a couple of years coaching Miami University's men's tennis team, and is now the USTA's Director of Multi-Cultural Development. Among other things, Rodney helps create programs that will attract more minorities to tennis.

I liked practicing with Rodney, who had a 6-foot, 2-inch wiry frame during his playing years. I knew if I could chase down and return his groundstrokes and serves, I'd be able to handle whatever any woman player could dish out. Still, having John and Willis as practice partners wasn't exactly a step down. They were smooth players who were in top shape at the time and used to work Lori and me to the point of exhaustion. They were great teachers, too.

Even when I was a junior, Willis gave me a few good pointers on how I could improve my serve. So I was eager to soak in whatever he had to say. We were like the four black musketeers with a one-for-all and all-for-one approach to everything we did.

Lori and I were inseparable during that time. We practiced together, watched each other's matches, and played doubles together until we were 21.

I won my first WTA Tour title in 1984; Lori got her first title in 1986. She earned that title by beating me 2–6, 7–5, 6–2 in a historic match. It was the first time two black female pros had met in the final of a tour event. It also was the first time Lori and I had played each other as pros. I had the blues after that loss because I had never lost to her in junior events.

I was steadier than Lori was from the baseline, but she was much quicker at the net and she loved to come in behind her serve. I believe she beat me in our first meeting as pros because she was more daring. She came to the net on anything, while I was hitting my passing shots with neither pace nor accuracy. Even when I stroked what I thought was a great passing shot, she was there to punch it away for a winner. She seemed to know where I was going even before I did. We called Lori "the cat" because of the way she lurked around the net. She hit volleys to die for. Lori and I were determined to prove that we belonged among the game's elite. Obviously, we succeeded. I reached a career high No. 4 in 1989; Lori reached a career high No. 9 in 1988.

Reminiscing about those earlier years, John sighed and said of Lori and me, "I never saw two girls with the heart and ability that those two girls had. Both of them had the ability to be No. 1 in the world. The young black girls I teach now don't have the focus they had. When Zina was 12, she had as strong a mind as any of the 18-year-old players."

Everything went smoothly with the musketeers until Lori's game took a dramatic jump. Because I had dominated her in the juniors, it was difficult for me to cope with even the thought of playing second fiddle to her as a pro. She beat me the first four times we played. I finally won my first pro match against her at the 1990 Virginia Slims of Chicago. She won our career head-to-head series, beating me in seven of twelve matches.

Lori got stronger and became more confident as she adjusted to life as a pro. At the same time, my confidence sagged. I was used to being the one in the limelight. I guess I felt threatened by Lori once she started beating me. I got paranoid, too. Whenever we played each other, it seemed to me that John and Willis were clapping for Lori and rooting for her more than they were for me.

The group split up after Lori reached the 1987 U.S. Open semifinals. We didn't part on good terms. Lori signed a contract with IMG and agreed to play doubles with Betsy Nagelsen, wife of IMG founder Mark McCormack. That was very disturbing to me because when Lori first came out on the tour, I basically supported her. Betsy offered her something like $30,000, through a patch deal, to play doubles with her. My thing was that we were No. 3 in the world and were going to make a lot more if we stayed together.

I felt miserable after Lori signed, but it helped me understand that not everyone saw things the way I did or had the same level of loyalty. I understood that Lori did what she believed she had to do. Still, I was very, very bitter with her for a very long time. It was a growing experience for us both, and I'm happy to say that we've moved on. We still spend time together, and we remain pretty good friends today after mending our relationship. We used to say we'd be sisters for life no matter what. We knew there might be some tough times, but I can honestly say that we've kept that pact.

Willis believed that Lori's father Charlie convinced her to break away from the group. "Lori's father felt that John couldn't coach both of them," he said. "How can you give two people in the top ten the time and energy they need? In hindsight, I can see that that's not possible. The group's camaraderie worked because not only did you have two players in the top ten, but they were also a top doubles team. The problem came when they played each other. They would look up in the stands and wonder which of them did John and I truly want to win."

John blamed himself for not showing us how to be fast friends as well as fierce competitors when we played each other as juniors.

"The best matches I've seen in my life were played when Lori and Zina went after each other in the finals of junior events," John said. "They would fight like cats and dogs. There were times when I just had to call it off. Even when they played practice matches, I would stop it at 5–all.

"I've often wondered if I should have stopped it then because later, when they played against each other as pros, it created all kinds of messes. I would tell them, 'We are all in this together. We all win. We are not trying to beat each other. That's not our objective.'

"But I should have gone further than that and helped them work out the emotions that emerged when they played each other."

After we split, I used to see Lori quite often at various events, but we didn't hang together like we used to. We stayed with our own separate groups. I never asked her about the circumstances surrounding her decision to sign with IMG. She talked about it recently. This is the way she saw it:

"I didn't really understand the whole thing, but a lot of things happened. One thing in particular was Mark McCormack asked me to play doubles with his wife Betsy in a couple of tour events, including two Grand Slam events. Looking back now, maybe it wasn't the best decision. I felt that Zina and I could play the other two grand slams, but she said she wouldn't play with me at all if I didn't agree to play doubles with her at every event."

That was her choice. But there was more to it.

Lori added: "Sometimes Zina and I played well together and sometimes we didn't. I felt a lot of pressure when I first started playing doubles with her because she was the higher-ranked player. I don't think I played that well when we started playing together. As I got more confidence as a singles player, we became a better team. But when I got better in singles, it became more competitive between us. At that time, she hadn't beaten me in singles, and I think that was affecting our play as doubles partners. I think every team with two top-ranked singles players has problems, but it was more difficult for us because our relationship went way back and we were like sisters. It just became too competitive."

I think the musketeers had a good run and we achieved a lot by working as a group. However, there were many times I didn't feel like I was part of a big, happy family. Having lost both parents prematurely to death and then having my best friend Lori walk away troubled me terribly. I felt the need to get away from John because I no longer wanted him to control my life. I asked Willis to coach me just before Lori asked him. That caused a problem because John thought Willis was doing things behind his back. It wasn't like that at all. John always wanted total control. As I got older, I wanted more freedom. I didn't think of Willis as a surrogate father the way I did with John, so I knew I wouldn't allow Willis to be as controlling as John was.

I remember once sitting in a room with John, Willis, and several other business advisors, discussing my decision to fire John. John is the kind of person who needs someone else to back him up, so he kept trying to get the others in the room to persuade me to stay with him. They told him that evidently I seemed to have made up my mind. I told John that I appreciated what he had done for me, but I needed to move on with my life. I cried all night after that meeting, but deep inside, I believed it was something that had to be done.

I guess I feel that while the musketeer concept helped Lori and me make it to the top in tennis, it stifled our development as young women. Basically, Lori and I were like robots during that time. We weren't supposed to do anything else but play tennis.

We had no social life. We couldn't have a boyfriend or go to parties. John used to say, "You don't need a boyfriend; you don't need to party. Your life is tennis." We rarely went to any of the Women's Tennis Association social affairs. We were told to go home, rest, then start the same routine the next day.

There's no doubt that there is an inherent loneliness in tennis. It's an individual sport, and it's hard to make relationships that are fulfilling when you're going out and competing against one another all the time. But the biggest thing I've learned since I've retired is that a lot of the relationships you make on the tour are lasting relationships because of all we go through together. After all the competition is over, we are friends on a deeper level.

I learned a lot about the importance of socializing and supporting the tour from Chris Evert, Martina Navratilova, and Pam Shriver when we were teammates on the U.S. Fed Cup team. They said that by attending the various WTA functions I helped promote myself as well as women's tennis. I developed a whole new perspective on the business side of tennis too. Being around Chris and Martina and observing how they were able to compete against each other and go through hard times yet stay friends also was enlightening. Had I been exposed to that earlier, maybe Lori and I would have stayed together.

I look back with no regrets, but I do feel like I missed out on some things. I'm not going to blame it totally on John because I understood that I had to give up a big chunk of my childhood to be a top pro. I knew my social life and everything else would have to take a back seat to tennis. Sure, I strayed from the straight and narrow every now and then, but John always put me right back on track after learning that I had violated his rules.

In some respects, I'm very happy with the way things turned out, but I sometimes wonder what would have happened if my relationship with John had been more balanced. John grew up during a time when young folks didn't talk back to their elders. His "my way or the highway" philosophy might have worked in his own day. Since I've been able to reflect on the whole experience, I'm afraid his way resembled what some now call mental abuse.

I think Andrea Jaeger and Roland Jaeger might have been the first and best example of an abusive father-daughter coaching relationship on the tour. Ranked No. 2 in the world in 1987, Andrea became the family breadwinner soon after she turned pro at 15. That's a lot of pressure to put on a child. I felt a lot of pressure when I was 21, even 30; a 15-year-old kid has got to feel it even more. You're expected to win and if you don't, you know that you might be depriving mom and dad of a new car or a house.

John recalls a nasty incident while I was playing Andrea in the final of a junior event in Birmingham, Alabama.

"Roland stood up in the middle of the match and told his daughter that if she didn't make the umpire overrule a call, he was going to pull her off the court. The umpire indeed overruled it, and everybody started booing."

When I was a junior, Andrea's father told John that I'd never be a tennis player because I didn't have a backhand. I never forgot that comment; it inspired me to work harder to improve my backhand. After I turned pro, I beat Andrea at the Virginia Slims in Houston.

The backhand turned out to be one of my best shots. When know-it-all Roland said I would never be a player, that gave me added incentive to prove something, not to him but to myself. I improved my backhand simply by hours and hours and hours and buckets and buckets and buckets of balls. I did it so many times it became second nature. I hit tens of thousands of balls; I hit until my hand was almost bleeding. I had callouses you wouldn't believe. I'm a perfectionist anyway, and a backhand is simply practice. Say something's my weakness and I'll try to make it so that you can't say it again. I created a backhand out of myself. I got comfortable by doing it over and over. Then, on the court ... backhand—no pressure. I know *that one.* You got anything better? Give me only backhands for all I care.

Andrea was 17 when she reached the 1982 French Open final and the 1982 Australian Open semifinal. Four years later a shoulder injury forced her off the tour. To put it bluntly, Andrea was a spoiled brat. She just expected everything to go her way. It's interesting to me to see now how much she has changed. She has become a very caring person and done a lot of good work through her children's foundation for terminally ill kids.

In recent years, the women's tour has received a great deal of bad press from other mentally or physically abusive father/daughter relationships. Mary Pierce, who won the 1995 Australian Open, suffered through some stormy times with her father Jim when he was her coach. Jim Pierce frequently attacked Mary verbally in public and sometimes would yell at her opponents during a match. He also was involved in a fist-fight with spectators at Roland Garros Stadium during one of Mary's French Open matches.

The WTA Tour banned him from all events for several years after that. Though the ban was lifted in 1998, their relationship remained strained.

Teen star Martina Hingis won three Grand Slam titles in 1997, including the Australian Open and Wimbledon. She and her mother, Melanie Molitor, seem to have a solid abuse-free relationship. But it's still too soon to know if it'll stay that way. When I first saw Martina come in the locker room during her rookie year, I was impressed with her attitude. She was eager to be a pro but comfortable with the fact that she still had the yearnings of a normal teenager. Her mother allowed her to practice with other women pros and didn't seem to be putting a lot of pressure on her to win. After Martina won the 1997 Australian Open, she went rollerblading along the Yarra River in Melbourne just like a normal teenager. I believe a mother-daughter coaching relationship is healthier, surely less intense, than a father-daughter one.

A female coach is going to be more sensitive to the emotional needs of a female player. A man has never played or lived in a woman's body; he can't understand what we go through. There are moods that we experience that only a woman can understand. Men just don't get it, and you really can't expect them to get it.

Women also don't get it with some of the things men do that we can't. For example, men can beat each other's brains out in athletic competition and afterwards go happily share a beer. A woman is likely to sulk. She might be pissed off because she doesn't like the skirt her opponent is wearing, or might decide that she wants to beat her opponent because her skirt is too short. After the match she might not want to speak to her opponent at all. That's just the way it is. Men get that it's just a game and, afterwards, they move on. That's not as easy for women to do.

I realize that tennis is a man's world, and in a way I understand the discipline and toughness that John and other male coaches try to develop in their female players. But girls are raised differently; many of us were never encouraged to develop athletic skills when we were very young, and we can't just be ordered to make up for lost time. As more female pro athletes become stars, I think the traditional way that girls have been raised will change for the better.

I admire women pros like Steffi Graf and Monica Seles who can shut out everything when they take the court. I don't believe most women can do that. Ironically, I was able to do it against Monica when I beat her in the '90 Wimbledon quarterfinals. I had the same take-no-prisoner attitude when I met Steffi that year in the semifinals.

# 12

# Fortnight to Remember, Semifinals

## *Garrison vs. Steffi Graf*

REMEMBER WHAT I SAID about my coach, Sherwood Stewart, looking at me like I was a nut when he learned that I was very superstitious? Remember his casual reaction to my insistence that we park in the same spot in the Wimbledon lot after I won my first-round match?

Well, after I beat Monica in the quarterfinals, Sherwood experienced a superstitious awakening of a sort. When we drove onto the Wimbledon parking grounds for my semifinal match against Steffi Graf, Sherwood jockeyed for "our" parking spot like a man possessed. He even yelled at a motorist angling for the same spot.

After I beat Monica, Sherwood actually wanted me to stay at home and go in hiding, just to make sure (ha!) that a black cat wouldn't cross my path. He didn't want me around if anybody in our group accidentally split any poles or walked under a ladder. Yeah, that's right. All of a sudden, he was the one acting like a nut.

I guess he figured I'd need a bunch of lucky charms and all the horseshoes in Texas to beat Steffi, who was the dominant women's pro in the late 1980s. In 1988, Steffi won the Golden Slam, which is the Australian Open, French Open, Wimbledon, U.S. Open, and the Olympic gold medal in singles. In 1989, she just missed winning a second consecutive Grand Slam by losing to Spain's Arantxa Sanchez Vicario 7–6, 3–6, 7–5 in the French Open final.

Steffi arrived at the 1990 Wimbledon as the top seed and two-time defending champion. She had beaten me the last five times we played. So why did I believe I could stop her from reaching her third consecutive Wimbledon final? Because I knew how to beat her and I had beaten her before.

Okay, Steffi was only 16 when I rallied to beat her 6–7, 6–1, 6–2 at the 1985 WTA Championship. Even then she whacked the hell out of the ball and played with that never-say-die attitude that's the mark of a champion. In our first encounter, she spent her energy trying to run down every shot, even those I knew were sure winners.

Back then, Steffi was just beginning to formulate and feel comfortable with the power game that prompted *Boston Globe* tennis columnist Bud Collins to dub her Fraulein Forehand. Still, it was clear to me that she was going to be something special. I just had no idea how special.

Though I played pretty good tennis during our first meeting, it was my experience that got me the win. I kept her off balance by mixing in a variety of spins and slices. She probably had never seen some of the junk I threw at her because she committed numerous unforced errors.

Obviously lacking confidence, Steffi kept scanning for her father/coach, Peter, who was moving from section to section in the stands, trying not to be detected giving her signals. Coaching on the pro tours while a match is in progress is prohibited, but some coaches, if they see their player struggling or playing without a clue, tend to ignore the rules.

Being seeded ahead of Steffi gave me another mental edge in that match. It's funny how the mind works. When you're a top seed, you believe you should beat any lower-ranked opponent you face. Sometimes you can sense that your opponent believes that too. Consequently, I got a few free points in that maiden match against Steffi from my reputation rather than my shot-making repertoire.

But once Steffi zoomed to the top, I became the lower-ranked player, the one giving up the free points when she stared at me from the other side of the net. I stayed close in several matches over the years against her, but most of the time, at 5–6 or 5–5, something would go awry. I'd miss a forehand, overhead, or some other easy shot.

I began most matches trying to gain an edge with my superior athleticism. That approach hardly works when the opponent is Graf, one of the sports world's most gifted woman athletes. Still, I've had my chances against the German superstar.

When I think about those lost opportunities against her, I recognize that I was always pressing. I have the ability to do just about anything I want with the ball, but oftentimes I made bad choices in my selection of shots. When I played Steffi, I just wanted to win so badly. I suspect that's why I played too cautiously.

I wouldn't use the word "choke," but someone told me that Billie Jean King used it to describe my demeanor during my match against Monica. Billie Jean also said that she didn't believe I'd be offended because we had talked about it over the years.

I'd be lying if I said the term didn't bother me. I'd just say that we all have different ways of dealing with pressure. I always felt I should do better against Steffi because Lori always played well against her. Even in losses, Lori made Steffi sweat. She pushed Steffi to the limit in the 1987 U.S. Open semifinal before losing in three tough sets. Actually, Lori might be the only player to have defeated Steffi in the first round of two major events: the 1992 Virginia Slims Championships and the 1994 Wimbledon.

On being able to handle Steffi's best stuff, Lori said, "What's the big deal? She has no backhand, so just play everything to her backhand and get to the net." Lori helped me see Steffi as a great tennis player, but someone who wasn't invincible. "Keep the pressure on her backhand and you'll beat her," Lori told me.

I've always admired Steffi as a person because mentally, I believe, she's one of the strongest people I've ever faced on a tennis court. She has gone through so much, with injuries and with her father Peter, who was jailed in Germany on tax-evasion charges. But when you faced her in a match, you'd never know she had anything on her mind but beating you to a pulp.

Emotionally, I'm just the opposite of Steffi. Arthur once noted that he could always tell when things weren't going well off the court with me or Yannick Noah by observing our on-court body language. Neither my body language nor my game betrayed me against Steffi that day.

I felt that if I were going to beat Steffi in a big match, it would happen on Wimbledon's Centre Court, where I felt so much at home. I was refreshed and relaxed when I woke up the morning of our match. I tried different rituals over the years, but nothing seemed as effective as the mental exercises I learned in therapy a few months before 1990's Wimbledon. Some people like to sit with their coach or a bunch of other people before a match and rehash an opponent's style and tendencies. I hate going over last-minute stuff like that. It's too much like cramming for a big classroom exam. I can't relax that way.

Through therapy, I learned to visualize myself executing the proper stroke or employing smart tactics on key points. While resting in bed or relaxing in the players' lounge, I would play matches in my mind. I'd battle an opponent in my mind's eye point by point, set by set. Sometimes I'd intentionally lose a point by hitting a short ball, then make the adjustment during the next imagined point. I learned to observe and track what happens to my body at stressful moments in a match and when to use conscious breathing to eliminate tension. Calmness under duress can be a mighty weapon.

I hit the ball crisply in practice, which was unusual for me. I struck it with even greater precision and purpose during the match. I took advantage of Steffi's second serves and rushed to the net at every opportunity. I also thought about Lori's advice and visualized flashbacks of the way I beat Steffi back in '85. I knew I had to hit well-angled crosscourt forehand groundstrokes to set up shots to her backhand. The trick was to be able to withstand the power from her forehand drives and to direct my returns toward her backhand, her weaker side. Of course, I mean "weaker" in comparison to the rest of her game. I'm sure many players would love to have Steffi's slice backhand. Dispatched with heavy underspin, it stays low. Which means you have to hit under the ball in order to make sure it clears the net on its return.

I had little trouble handling Steffi's slice during that match. After all, I like low balls—more direct shots, where I drive through the ball. I don't like balls that come up and over head-on. I'm short and small. Higher balls are hard for me to hit. Balls that are low play to my strength.

I know I'll never forget match point.

My mind was focused, and my arms were very loose. I served an ace down the middle, just inside the service line, then raced to the net with both arms extended, jumping for joy. I've never been more excited or more pleased about my performance at any other time in my life. Little Zina had finally advanced to the Wimbledon final. And she did it in grand style, upsetting top-seeded Steffi Graf 6–3, 3–6, 6–4.

In her post-match interview, Steffi said she believed I was going to fall apart at the end. She said, "I was ready to go for every shot and I knew I was going to get some shots, but she didn't miss, she didn't make any mistakes like she had done before. She played well to the end. She had great concentration."

Responding to HBO's Larry Merchant, I said, "I stuck to the game plan that Sherwood and I had discussed before I went out there. Any time I had a chance to get in, I got in. I did the things I knew I could do and didn't try to do the things I couldn't do."

Asked about Willard's influence, I said, "Willard is a very positive person, and a lot of that has come to me."

Before the tournament I promised everyone we'd fly back on the Concorde if I won the title. That night I thought I was going to have to pay up.

Even when I was a junior, I had dreamed of playing in a Wimbledon final. I could see myself holding the winner's trophy above my head, smiling before a throng of cameras. It was hard to believe that I was one match away from realizing my ultimate dream. Just getting to the final was big news everywhere. Little did I know that beating Steffi would lead to the big-bucks deals that had eluded me most of my career.

I never thought about the importance of beating Steffi until Bryant Gumbel, who was then co-host of NBC's "Today" show, mentioned that I had a chance to make history by becoming the first African-American woman to win a Wimbledon singles title since Althea Gibson did it in 1957–58.

A couple of Houston television stations considered sending correspondents over just to interview me, but I don't believe they did.

I was like, 'Hey, they never paid any attention to me before, what's going on?' A London tabloid paid Willard $15,000 for an exclusive interview about our lives, how we met, etc. It was a little bitty article. That's when I understood that I had done something a bit unusual. But that was just the beginning.

Patrick came by that night to let me know that Reebok had agreed to give me a three-year shoes and clothing endorsement deal. That was great, but it posed a problem because I had to agree immediately to wear the Reebok line against Martina in the final.

I represented Martina's line designed by her companion, Judy Nelson. When I initially talked to Martina about wearing her outfits, I agreed—without pay—to start at Wimbledon. An agreement without compensation might not have been the smartest way to go. But what choice did I have?

I was pleased that I could help Martina by endorsing her clothing line.

Indeed, it's disgraceful that a woman who won fifty-six Grand Slam titles in her twenty-year pro career, a woman who is considered to be one of the game's all-time greats, retired in 1994 without ever having a major clothing manufacturer offer her an endorsement.

Evidently, Madison Avenue didn't believe Martina's lesbian lifestyle would sell on Main Street USA. A lot of people didn't even understand why I wore her clothes. My thing was, what's the big deal? I didn't have any clothes to wear, she was trying to promote Judy's line, and we were good friends. I didn't see anything wrong with doing it. I wasn't getting bought; I did it out of friendship.

I go straight at things, which is very difficult at times for other people. I have trouble handling the force of my own energy. My biggest strengths sometimes turn out to be weaknesses as well. I'm always battling between the two. My greatest asset is being able to analyze a situation and look at it for what it is. Once I've decided something, there's no stopping me. It may take me a while to fight the battle and decide, but once I decide, it's total straight-ahead.

As delighted as I was about getting a long-overdue endorsement deal with a major firm, I hesitated just a bit this time. I felt that Martina's outfits had been lucky and I didn't want to change my luck. In addition, Martina and Judy weren't exactly thrilled about me dropping them at the time because they were about to launch the clothing line nationally.

Patrick let me know that Martina had promised to pay a guarantee if I stayed with them. Then Octagon's Phil de Picciotto told Martina that I was receiving other offers and we needed written confirmation on that guarantee. At that point, which was the night before the final, they couldn't do it. It was an awfully difficult time because I think they thought we were engaging in some kind of gamesmanship before the match. But it was also strictly a business decision; I felt we had to take advantage of the opportunity, even though it might annoy my opponent as well as the gods of good fortune who had been so kind to me throughout the tournament.

Patrick also negotiated patch deals for me with S. Oliver, a German jeans company, Sun-Maid Raisins, and Budget Rental Cars. He even got Sherwood a hat deal with a fishing company.

Though I continued to play with my Wilson racket at Wimbledon, I signed a long-term deal with Yonex a bit later. My second week of competition neared an end with me still in contention for a mixed doubles title, too. Ricky Leach and I beat Jim Pugh and Jana Novotna 7–6 (10–8), 7–6 (7–4) to advance to the mixed doubles final, but Patty Fendick and I lost to Novotna and Helena Sukova 7–6 (7–1), 6–4 in the women's doubles semifinals.

By the way, Willard gave me two dogs after we got home. I named one Wimbly and the other one I called Ace to remind me of the ace I hit at match point with Steffi.

The attention I got for reaching the singles final was mind-boggling. You lose a lot of that front-runner support when you're not in contention on the final day.

It's taken me quite a while, but I finally understand that the most important person to satisfy is yourself, not your family, friends, or fans. You've got to be happy with your own self-image and not worry about how you think others might see you.

Believe me, it's not easy to do. You might say I'm talking with been-there, done-that insight. I've come to appreciate the importance of developing strong self-esteem because mine was so low for so long. Even after I had reached my first Wimbledon final by beating Steffi, I wasn't totally happy with my life. Despite my popularity and all my other successes, I've never felt really good, really comfortable with myself. Like several other celebrities I know, I suffer from an illness that I kept hidden from the public's eye most of my career. It's a scary disease. Some of your family members or close friends might have it as well, and you'd never know. If they do, they're probably too ashamed to talk about it. I sure was.

# 13

## Battling Bulimia

How would you feel if you stood naked before a mirror and thought your buns looked as big and round as extra-large beachballs, connected to thighs as massive as Lake Michigan? While Kim Carnes was singing about white girls having Bette Davis eyes in 1981, I felt like a funny-looking black girl who played tennis with Houston running back Earl Campbell's thighs. Wouldn't be the best way to start your day, would it? Made me want to puke every day.

Actually, if you're bulimic—as I am—you tend to feel that vomiting after every meal is the thing to do to look slim and pretty. Many of an estimated two to three million people who suffer from this eating disorder have similar feelings. Most bulimics are actually young white females. Strivers. Strong and ambitious women who have done well in this male-dominated world. I suspect I am among only a few blacks who don't quite fit the government-approved profile. What can I say?

I was a highly successful and popular black woman athlete who never liked the image I saw staring back at me from a mirror. Even as a child, I found a full-length view of my naked body a painful sight.

At age 12, I was considered big compared to the white girls I competed against in 12-and-under junior tournaments; in fact, you may remember I was accused of lying about my age. While others were bothered that I might be too old, I would have been glad for any excuse for my bulk. I noticed all the white girls' figures and admired how slim they looked in their tennis outfits. I never realized then that the people who made those tiny shirts and skirts fashioned them specifically for slender white women, not black women with big butts like mine. I often got quite frustrated trying to stuff my body into the outfits available.

I've had concerns about my size and weight ever since I started playing tennis. The older I got, the more of a problem it became, especially after I got acquainted with junk food. My weight got out of control a couple of times when I was a junior. Since I never saw a fat person excel on the tennis court, I knew the extra pounds had to go. I learned how to get rid of them—and have my pizza, too—while visiting relatives during a trip to California. A female cousin told me all I had to do was stick my hand down my throat after every meal and I could eat as much as I wanted. I thought that was something I should try. So I did and it worked. I did it for a while, then stopped when I felt I had my weight in check.

My urge to binge and purge returned when mama died. There was an emptiness inside me I needed to fill. It seemed like I never had enough to eat, and I believed that no one other than mama cared about me as a person. Everyone else idolized a tennis player. Before I knew it, I was binging and purging nearly every day. I did it for three straight years.

I felt the need to purge whenever John would criticize me about not hustling on court, or for failing to hit a dozen perfectly placed forehands down the line, or after losing a match that he felt I shouldn't have lost. I'd deal with the crisis afterwards by eating a medium pizza all by myself. Then I'd spend the rest of the night trying to get rid of it. It's something you do in the privacy of your bathroom, but you can also do it on a plane or in a restaurant if necessary. Strangers would ask me if I was okay after I'd emerge from an airplane restroom with bloodshot eyes and a haggard look.

For a long time, I barfed every time I ate anything that I knew I should avoid. Junk food, pizza, hot dogs, potato chips, and Captain Crunch cereal were high on my no-no list. After a while, it was easy for me to purge any food except pizza, chocolate, or cheese. I needed to drink a lot of fluids before purging those things. I'd throw up, drink a little water; throw up again, then drink more water. You learn little tricks and other methods of purging. Most of the time, I'd use my fingers; other times, I was able to throw up just by thinking about how bad I felt.

I knew when I had gained too much weight not just by the way my clothes fit but by the comments people made. Think about it. When you're trim and slim people will flat-out say, "My, you look great!" But when you've gained a few pounds, people don't say a word. They just give you that look. Later, they'll tell their friends about how fat you are.

Purging isn't a very comfortable feeling. But it's a point of control. You feel like you're getting something out of you on your own. You stick your hand down your throat and you make something happen; you control your own insides. The funny thing is: the more you do it, the further you have to stick your hand down. It takes greater stimulation.

In the African-American community a lot of people think bulimia is a disease that you catch. Someone has bulimia like a flu. But it's not a bug; it's something you inflict on yourself—very close to being a drug addict. The majority of the time you feel that everything around you is out of control, and this is one place where you can get some kind of control. It's a very powerful raw addiction: *I control my guts. I control the way food goes in and out of me.* Very basic.

Bulimia can cause hair loss, soft nails, dehydration, stomach ulcers, tooth decay, and heart palpitations. I get shivers thinking about the first time I experienced an irregular heartbeat. Willard and I were attending a Houston Rockets game, and I thought I was going to die. I had eaten a slice of pizza and just as quickly went to the bathroom to get rid of it. It was a close, exciting game, and I jumped from my seat several times clapping and screaming support. When my heart started to race, I sat down abruptly. Willard asked if I was okay. I told him I felt my heart moving, but I didn't tell him about purging the pizza.

The next day, a doctor told me I'd be okay and that I should try not to get upset so much. I couldn't believe, as frantic as I felt, that that was all he could think to say: "Don't be stressed."

"My life is stress," I screamed.

My life at the time was indeed as bad as living gets. My husband was telling me he'd be willing to start a family if I stayed on the tour one more year. In the meantime, he was spending my money to have an affair with one of my friends. And for more than a year, I listened to that same husband repeatedly tell me he thought I was fat and ugly.

How could this doctor expect me not to be upset? 'It's a little too late for that, buddy,' I thought.

I'll have more to say about life with Willard later.

It took me a while to understand that low self-esteem is bulimia's best buddy. Naturally, if you think you're fat and ugly, your self-esteem hangs out in the toilet with the rest of the waste. Striving to be perfect and falling short contributes to low self-esteem as well. Most people with bulimia are never satisfied with their achievements. They don't take the time to savor their victories and successes; they push on to the next challenge. I know that's what I do.

I sometimes sink into an abnormally deep funk when rejection or depression slaps me in the face. One of my worst woe-is-me episodes came about because of an injury I suffered while playing in Europe. I stopped tennis for a while because of pain that was later diagnosed as a stress fracture in my toe.

I have trouble anyway playing through injuries. Some people can have a major knee problem and, if it doesn't hurt too bad, they can play. If I felt a twitch, it sometimes wrecked my whole game. But I was always very truthful. John's doubting me made me think that tennis the game was more important to him than Zina the person. Did Zina exist only when she was on the court? But Zina on the court was a version of Zina the human being. Tennis was simply one of Zina's ways of expressing herself, and the integrity and fire of her game were based on the integrity and fire of her person. If you're going against that, you're going against my character, the way I am, the whole nine yards.

John intimidated me, and I didn't know what to do or say. I was sure he thought I was lying and didn't want to play. I felt totally hurt because I was telling the truth, but no one believed me. So I went home to binge and purge for two weeks. I remember eating cereal, pizza, and fried chicken, and just throwing up nonstop. It felt so good feeling bad that I extended my home visit by two more weeks. That was a really tough period professionally because I missed the French Open and Wimbledon.

Another tough period occurred when I was preparing to play an event in Houston. I was always stressed about playing at home, mainly because I always put more pressure on myself there. This time, the pressure was unreal. I felt like I didn't want to live anymore. I didn't want the pressure, and I didn't want anyone around me. I felt totally bereft.

Bulimia always got me into a self-destructive cycle. Week after week in town after town, I'd practice, play my match, go to my room, eat, and purge. I didn't want to be around anybody. I just wanted to disappear. Instead of gaining confidence, I lost it. Bulimia works on your mind, makes you paranoid. You think everybody is watching you.

I never again saw or talked to the cousin who gave me my first lesson in binging and purging, but I became an expert on my own. Bulimia is a very private thing that you don't discuss. You can do it for a long time without people noticing. George Kennard, my child-hood friend, was the only person who knew I was binging and purging as a teenager. He used to hear me throwing up in the bathroom after I'd eat. He told me to seek help.

Once when I was in London, I lost a cap on a tooth. The dentist who put it back on guessed what was happening. I pretended I didn't know what he was talking about. When you throw up a lot, the acids from your stomach eat away the enamel on your teeth. Dentists can tell instantly.

Other weird things started happening. My veins started showing around my eyes. My hair got very thin and started falling out, and I got blotches on my face. When I had to play Chris Evert in a nation-ally televised match, I remember trying to explain the blotches away by saying that it was fungus. I was more worried about people notic-ing the spots on my face than I was about beating Chris.

I won that day, but the illness caused me to lose several matches to less talented players. I lost a match to somebody ranked No. 200-plus in the world because I had no energy. I had squandered my ability to survive tough fights, my gift from the bayou.

That's when I decided to reveal my secret to John. He didn't have a clue what I was talking about. He took me to the WTA Tour trainer, who found a doctor for me to see in Houston.

People prone to suffer with bulimia mostly are normal-weight, high-achieving, passive women with troubled backgrounds—per-fectionists. An exact cause isn't known, but researchers believe that rejection, loss of family members, and a pervasive sense of failure are some of the co-factors.

Many famous people, including movie stars, professional athletes, and gymnasts, are bulimia sufferers. In my case, purging was more about believing I was ugly compared to white female players while feeling unloved and wanting to be perfect in everything I did than it was about being actually overweight.

Bulimia is not the same as anorexia. In anorexia a person seems to want to starve to death. Carling Bassett, a former pro from Canada, admitted that she suffered from anorexia, but she never discussed her situation in depth back then (though she may have since). I believe other tennis pros suffered with anorexia, but they kept it hidden. I once developed symptoms of anorexia. I just kind of shut down and stopped eating in 1985 when I played Chris in the Amelia Island final. I was binging and purging, but I would only eat lettuce or broccoli. When it got to the point where I wouldn't eat at all, John used to make me eat. That's the closest I've ever been to that condition.

Bulimia is also not something that just started in the era of looking at magazines and trying to be as thin as you can. It's old. It's a natural human act of some sort, even if a self-destructive one. It's as old as the human race. It touches on some kind of primal human drive, maybe an urge for self-destruction or a form of shame. But it also could be an expression of power and privilege. I read somewhere that kings who lived centuries ago would eat and eat and then throw up.

Anyway, binging and purging are definitely out there to do, and you have to pay close attention to your kids because they could be doing it and you wouldn't even know. They are absolutely a part of women's sports, but no one really pays that much attention to it. It's a disease that no one wants to discuss because people tend to think you're crazy for doing that to yourself.

I first disclosed that I was bulimic in 1989 in a *Sports Illustrated* feature story about me. I got a lot of instant feedback from mothers of young girls who admitted that either they or their daughters— or both!—were doing it, too. I was especially shocked when a couple of men approached me to say they did it for a while. One of them was black. Overall, I heard from hundreds of people—mostly white women and Asian women—after that story came out.

During my first visit to a therapist, when asked to do a self-portrait, I drew an elephant. That's what I saw. Later, in another therapy session with six other people, I discovered to my astonishment that, in a way, I was no different from the drug addict sitting on my right or the executive on my left. I don't know what a junkie feels when he's doing drugs because I've never used them, but bulimia seems to be a comparable form of addiction. It makes you calm, at least for a while. Until the acid starts eating at your stomach lining. When that happened to me, I started doing laxatives. I lived on Exlax for a long time. I'd be lying if I said I still didn't use Exlax.

I found out through therapy that because of the loss of my father at an early age, I developed a feeling that everyone close to me was going to abandon me. That feeling was intensified when my mother died.

People would often tell me that I looked good, but it wouldn't register. While I got a high from them saying it, deep down inside I didn't believe them. At that time in my life, my tennis ranking was steadily going up, but I still felt very lonely, withdrawn. People thought I was shy when they met me, but a lot of it had to do with my being so insecure. I knew what I was accomplishing and, on every level other than athletic success, which I could achieve by agility and stamina, I wasn't comfortable with myself at all.

Bulimia is something you might try to control, but there's no cure for it. It's like being an alcoholic. I think I might have some inner stomach problems now because of the many times I spent in bathrooms everywhere tossing my cookies. I'm sure I have an ulcer, but I'm afraid to have tests to check. Bulimia alone will put you in a hospital bed, and I know some people have died from it. My situation has been partially controlled through therapy. I have learned to live with the desire to binge every day.

Having to pay $125 for every therapy visit also helped convince me that this was something I could lick. I didn't want to spend the rest of my life dishing out that much money to try to correct this problem. Through therapy, I started to meet people who openly talked about their issues. It helped to know that others had the same problem. Once I understood that bulimia was about suppressed anger, loneliness, and a feeling of abandonment, I grew more confident about controlling it. I started to do better.

The therapy helped me change the way I looked at things in my life. I was having a very hard time dealing with all of the pressures—from my mother dying, from being driven by a strong need to win, from supposedly being the next Althea Gibson, from not having any major endorsements, and from having to be a role model. And most of all, I felt pressure from just the everyday life of being black and trying to survive in a white world.

I've come to realize that my life and the lives of most people consist of a continuous flow of ups and downs. I've learned to put this problem and all others in the hands of God and not the next donut.

Relying on faith means that God will help me through. I face each problem as what it is and deal with it in that way, knowing that God will lead me out of it. I use prayer. I meditate on the situation. I also try to find scriptures in the Bible to help me.

I believe God expects us to take care of our bodies. In Corinthians 6:19, He says that our bodies are the temple of the Holy Ghost. Now that I'm older, I try to cope with my illness in a more spiritual way. I believe that I should love my body the way God loves me.

The bathroom is often the place I'll retreat into because it's private and secure. Some people use closets to pray. I'll use a closet sometimes too.

Close the door. Complete darkness. Sit over the tub. Or kneel down. Sometimes I see a flow of the most incredible purples and pinks. I've been told that's my aura. The colors are very calming; they relax and relieve me. I forget all the tension in my own body; stress melts into colors.

It doesn't mean that I get an answer or that my problem's going to leave that day. The answer can come two months from now, a year from now. That's where faith comes in, believing and knowing that God will have an answer to my problems.

And I don't always get the answer I want. It's not a negotiation; it's definitely a surrender. The more that I rely on my faith in God, the stronger my faith becomes. And that always means to let go— of a fearful state, an unknown. You can't let go if you don't have faith in God. Yet when you surrender, you automatically are set free.

I felt a similar kind of peace of mind and control at the 1990 Wimbledon, the night before meeting Martina in the final. Life for me definitely was on an upswing then. To have beaten Monica in the quarterfinals and Steffi in the semifinals was *almost* as good as it could get. I was determined to make it a wee bit better.

Little Zina from Houston was going for the big one—Wimbledon—against one of the game's greats—Martina Navratilova. I felt a match away from fulfilling the childhood dream that had driven me since my early days at MacGregor Park.

As the Winans put it: *"Millions didn't make it,/but I was one of the ones that did."*

# 14

# Fortnight to Remember, Final

## Garrison vs. Martina Navratilova

S HE WAS A LEFTY; I was a righty. She was white; I was black. She was born in the Czech Republic; I was born in Houston, Texas. We had opposite personalities.

I think it's safe to say that the story lines between the final two contestants for the 1990 Wimbledon crown were pretty sharp. Yet, in some ways, Martina Navratilova and I were cut from similar cloth. My father died when I was just a baby. Martina lost hers in a divorce when she was three. We were both tomboys. I played baseball and ran track against boys; she played soccer and ice hockey with boys.

In her book *Martina* (Ballantine Books, 1985) my opponent noted that when she looked at herself in a full-length mirror, she saw someone with big calves, big ears, and big feet. She cried because she felt she looked like a boy. I, on the other hand, drew pictures of elephants.

We both learned to play tennis when we were 10. Martina turned pro in 1975, seven years before I did. We became pretty good friends, but I'll forever remember Martina as the villain of my professional career. Nearly every time we played she beat my brains out.

She gave me a glimpse of what I had to look forward to during my rookie year when she thrashed me in the 1982 French Open quarterfinals. She gave me another whipping three weeks later in the Wimbledon fourth round.

I nearly always ended up on her side of the draw, which meant we'd meet before the final. Before the '90 Wimbledon, she had beaten me ten times in the quarterfinals of tour events, twelve times in the semifinals and four times in the final. In fact, before meeting in the 1990 Wimbledon final, Martina had beaten me in 27 of our 28 career matches.

I preferred to meet Chris Evert because I knew Chris was just going to sit back at the baseline and hit the ball back to me until I made a mistake. I knew she wasn't going to charge the net or go for winners. I always felt if I played well, I had a good shot against Chris, but Martina could just blow you off the court regardless of how well you were playing.

The women's final usually is played on the second Saturday of the two-week event. But a rainy second week, combined with my success in singles, doubles, and mixed doubles, forced officials to move the women's final to Sunday. Martina and I played right before Stefan Edberg met Boris Becker in the men's final.

I didn't cook on the eve of my playing Martina. Instead, Patrick invited twenty people for dinner at Fontana di Trevi, an upscale Italian restaurant in London. Chef Marcello prepared an assortment of delicious dishes. It felt great being waited on.

An aggressive serve-and-volleyer, Martina was always a tough person for me to play because she was a bit stronger and always seemed to be in better shape than I was. My matches against her routinely were lopsided. Whenever I took a break from the tour and stayed at home for a while, some friends would say stuff like, "If we could just get rid of Martina, you could be No. 1."

At one point, I told myself that if I could learn to hate her, maybe I could beat her. I actually tried to think of reasons I should hate her. Because of the type of person I am, that just didn't work. Each time

I tried to play with this hate thing, I'd go out on the court tense and uptight and play worse.

I got my only career victory over Martina in the 1988 U.S. Open. I beat her 6–4, 6–7 (3–7), 7–5 in the quarterfinals. I prepared for that event by working with Joe Breedlove, Martina's former trainer. I got to know Joe, an African-American from Dallas, while he still worked for Martina. The few blacks who were a part of the women's tour at the time frequently spent their social time together. We were able to reach a comfort level with each other that we can't reach when whites are among us. In an all-black environment, we know we can kick back and not worry about being judged. Think about this: If you're a white person at an all-black social affair, you're apt to perk up a bit if another white person shows up. Been there, done that? Then you know what I'm talking about.

When Joe stopped working for Martina, I hired him. Joe helped me improve my speed by having me run short and long sprints. My favorites were the 50- and 100-yard dashes, but I also did 220s, 440s, and 600s.

He played mind games with me. If I ran a 220 in 28 seconds, he'd tell me Martina did it in 27 seconds. My ego would get me every time he'd make those comparisons because I was considered the quickest player on tour. I wasn't about to let Martina, Steffi, or anybody else take that unofficial title from me.

For months, Joe and I ran laps together. Afterwards, he would say that I was a little faster than Martina or that I did this better than Martina or I did that better than Martina. I went to the '88 U.S. Open psyched and in the best shape of my life. Before I met Martina in the quarterfinals, Joe reminded me that I routinely beat her time in the 220s and that I was just as strong and fit as she was.

I played as if I were the superior player during the first set and a half. Then I must have had a flashback of the way it always had been against Martina. She got back into the match winning the second tiebreak in a breeze. I took charge in the final set, jumping to a 5–1 lead. But Martina came charging back. I kept telling myself that I couldn't get this close and let it slip away. When she tied the score at 5–5, I played more aggressively, charging the net on nearly every shot. You have to take the net away from Martina. If you don't, she'll be all over you like green on grass. I truly believe that I held Martina off because Joe convinced me that I had about a bare inch of a psychological edge over her. That victory made a lot of people happy, some of whom I didn't think knew anything about me or tennis.

That night, as I walked down the street from the Plaza Hotel, I noticed a homeless person holding a cup out, silently begging for money. When I passed by, he said, "Zina Garrison, great match. I'm proud of you." My lesson for that day was: being homeless doesn't mean you're clueless about what's going on in the world.

When I met Martina in the '90 Wimbledon final, I was as fit as I was when I beat her at the '88 U.S. Open. I knew I could do it again. After upsetting Monica Seles and Steffi Graf, two of the best players in the world, I went into the match with an I-can-do-it-one-more-time attitude.

Actually, I felt more pressure about being the first black woman to reach the Wimbledon final in thirty-two years than I did about facing someone I'd beaten only once before. I believe the All England Club sponsored Althea Gibson's trip to Wimbledon that weekend in anticipation of me making a bit of history. You wouldn't believe how nervous I felt just knowing that that tough, charismatic lady would be watching.

I was fine until Althea walked on the court during one of my warm-up sessions. Just seeing her and thinking about what she had achieved on this same court caused me to sweat. Her presence made me realize that I had an opportunity to do something that would make history.

After practice, Althea followed me into the locker room and started reminiscing. I never saw her play live or on television. Old-timers who saw her raved about how great she was in her prime. She endured so much before accomplishing her goals.

She pointed to the bathroom stall she used, and she showed me the little corner she rested in before playing her final match. She said she sat there, just getting her thoughts together. I was like, "Oh shit." All of a sudden I felt my heart pounding. The only thing she actually told me to do was to get out there and go for it.

I was twelve when I watched Arthur beat Jimmy Connors in the 1975 Wimbledon final. Then a commentator for HBO, Arthur flashed an excited grin each time I saw him at the '90 Wimbledon. "Hit that slice backhand," Arthur advised me before the final, "and just hang in there."

It felt great knowing that Althea and Arthur, the only blacks to win Wimbledon singles titles, would be among the Centre Court crowd pulling for me to win.

Later, I learned that my family back in Houston had gathered at my sister Clara's house to watch the match. They even invited Houston reporters and television crews to join them in an all-you-can-eat soul-food banquet.

I had mixed feelings about facing Martina that year because of our personal and business relationships. She was especially nice to me during the two weeks. Before each of my previous six matches, she and her coach, Craig Kardon, gave me scouting reports on my opponents and wished me good luck.

I had been wearing her clothing line during the entire tournament. Since we both reached the final, Martina's clothing line got quite a bit of exposure. However, I didn't wear one of her outfits when we met in the final.

Within hours of my victory against Graf in the semifinals, Reebok had signed me to that lucrative deal. The agreement called for me to wear Reebok clothes in the final against Martina. I'll have more to say about the mess that caused later.

I took the court wearing my new Reebok outfit. I was told that Chris Evert, who was a NBC commentator, noted my change of attire by saying, "Zina's got a new look today."

I doubt if many people realized that I was without an endorsement deal and would have had no line to represent if I hadn't agreed to wear Martina's clothes at Wimbledon. In his book *Days of Grace,* which was published a few months after he died, Arthur had this to say about why corporate America snubbed me:

"Then we have the example of Zina Garrison. Garrison was once the only player in the top 10 in the world who could not find a corporate sponsor. In her case, she was penalized not for bad behavior or bad publicity, but for 'bad' skin. She is black."

I could hardly breathe before the match began, but once I hit the first ball I felt fine. I really felt good until I muffed an opportunity to break Martina's serve with the score tied at 4–4. I had a backhand in the middle of the court and just launched it. Martina won the first set 6–4 and then got more aggressive. She just took me apart. She had been in that kind of situation many times before. And it showed. I was playing my first Grand Slam final, and my nerves got worse and worse and worse. It showed. Martina won the second set in a breeze, 6–1. Steffi and Martina were the only two players who might have been stronger athletes than I was. I could never maneuver them into a situation that they couldn't handle. No matter how well or how poorly you play, losing always sucks. Still, I was happy for Martina.

That victory gave her a record nine Wimbledon titles.

I wish people had the chance to know the real Martina and not the public figure that she appears to be. She's a fine, compassionate person inside, but because so many unjust things in her life have hurt her, she can be a little bit mean to people. I wish she would lighten up and take it one day at a time.

I understand the pain she has gone through wanting to be accepted despite being gay; yet I don't necessarily agree with her when she says gays and blacks are put in the same category by society. When

*Classic me: stubbornness, willpower, determination—at the 1990 Wimbledon finals.*

I walk into a restaurant and get snubbed or mistreated, people do that because they see that I am black. Martina could walk into the same restaurant and receive great service from people who dislike gays because they can't tell by looking at her that she's gay.

The gay lifestyle is one of those seldom-discussed issues of concern on the women's tour. A lot of parents of young women pros, especially fathers, still fear that hordes of lesbian players will try to approach their daughters in the showers.

I remember when I was much younger, John used to tell Lori and me to just go in the locker room, get dressed, and get out. He would get mad with Lori because she liked to hang out.

One time, another teenage pro and I walked into the locker room and saw Renee Richards standing in front of a mirror with nothing on. Renee, who once was a man named Richard Raskind, had a sex-change operation in August 1975 and later was allowed to join the women's pro tour.

Well, we looked at Renee, looked at each other, and then ran out of there like somebody was chasing us with a baseball bat. John saw the other girl running as fast as she could and wanted to know what was wrong with her. I was so taken aback, I couldn't explain at first; I couldn't find the words, but I finally got it out. John looked as though he were either aghast or about to laugh.

I was never approached by a gay player, but a woman news reporter came on to me when I was in my early twenties. It happened at the U.S. Open. I'll never forget it. She asked me if I wanted to spend the evening with her that night and I just said no. I couldn't believe it was happening to me.

When Martina first started dating Judy Nelson, the media—especially the London tabloids—were frantic about getting pictures of them together. Someone at a tournament in Eastbourne, England, offered me $10,000 to take a picture of Martina and Judy hugging or kissing. I said, "No way!" People would do anything to take away someone else's privacy.

Forming friendships with gay people was never a problem for me because I have people in my family who are gay. I've always been comfortable with my own sexuality, and I never considered changing. My attitude has always been if that's what a person wants or needs to do, that's okay. God loves us all, and he loves our different ways.

I remember Martina and I talking about being in love when she was with Judy and I was with Willard. I found it interesting that the problems she and Judy were facing were similar to those Willard and I were trying to resolve.

During my early years on tour, the gay presence was very strong. Everywhere you looked, you came in contact with someone gay. It was definitely a stressful time, especially when you lost. Some girls tried to get too friendly when they thought someone might be emotionally vulnerable. But in the '90s, I believe the total number of gays on the tour declined. Now you see more married couples with children traveling together.

Even though Chris Evert didn't have kids until after she retired, I think she set an example and showed that it was possible to do it all—be a professional athlete, be feminine, have a husband, kids, as well as explore other business interests. No one was doing that when I first came on tour.

The only time I feel uncomfortable is when I'm put in a situation where I am prejudged. If I traveled with a girlfriend before I was married, people would say, "What's up with that?" But they don't ask that kind of question when two guys are friends and travel together.

What I didn't like about the tour situation then was if you didn't have a relationship with a guy, or somebody didn't know that you liked guys, people just assumed you were gay because you were a tennis player. That stereotypical thing plagues women athletes because we're muscular and can compete as well as men. In any type of sport, we are thought of as being gay first and then a woman—until we prove otherwise.

That has always bothered me because I've considered myself to be extremely feminine. I mean, despite the cultural clichés, there's not just one way to be feminine. A female cheetah or eagle doesn't put on frilly airs.

I never had to worry about the London tabloids prying into my private life because, at the time, Willard and I were not a wild and crazy couple. In fact, a number of good things came together for me at that Wimbledon, thanks to Willard. He worked hard to keep all potentially bad stuff far away from me.

I never allowed him to get involved with my coaching because I felt that was my area and I was the one who had to work with the person I chose to coach me. Willard did help me understand that since I had a coach, a trainer, and a sports therapist on my payroll, I should listen to their recommendations. If I did otherwise, I shouldn't expect to get the maximum out of my game and the most for my money. I did that and it worked.

Despite falling a victory short of paradise, everything jelled quite well during Wimbledon that year. Some people believed that I fell short because I was satisfied just being a finalist. That wasn't the case at all. I would trade in all the endorsement deals, headlines, and everything else for the sheer joy and headiness that come with being a Wimbledon champion, with getting to hold up that plate. But the fallout from being the Avis of the 1990 Wimbledon wasn't too shabby.

# 15

# Wimbledon Aftermath

I F YOU'RE BLACK and ranked among the top ten players in the world, nearly everyone who follows the game knows your name.

Earn a berth in the Wimbledon final and it seems like most of the sports world wants to share your fame. I arrived in Los Angeles soon after Wimbledon, delighted to discover that my run armed me with the clout of a superstar. As I walked through L.A. International, people whispered my name. Some asked for autographs. That night, Willard and I scored a table at a posh L.A. restaurant without a reservation and without having to stand in a long line. I've been told that in Tinseltown, you've really got to be somebody or know somebody to be able to do that.

The instant recognition and red-carpet treatment touched me deeply. Still, I knew the good times wouldn't last forever.

Until that day came, Patrick encouraged me to strike while the iron was red-pepper hot. From the moment I beat Steffi Graf that Thursday in the Wimbledon semifinals, to the time I met Martina Saturday in the final, Patrick and his Octagon colleagues pulled together several lucrative endorsement deals and exhibitions.

With just a couple hours of sleep during a forty-eight-hour period, Patrick scrambled to nail down pacts with several corporations.

Thanks to Patrick, I also received a sizeable increase in appearance-fee checks from tennis promoters seeking my participation at exhibitions.

Recalling hours that were as full as whole days, Patrick observed, "From almost the moment Zina beat Steffi until 3:30 the morning of the final—which was almost two days later—I literally was on phone lines, trying to close deals before the final. Other Octagon staff members around the world were doing the same thing. The hardest part was arranging for Reebok's clothes and other companies' patches to arrive in England before the final. It's tough to get Saturday deliveries, even in London."

Patrick, no doubt about it, was the key to my Wimbledon payoff. But when I consider the toll it took on me physically, I sometimes wonder if it was worth it.

A few weeks before Wimbledon, I had agreed to play Monica Seles in an exhibition in Belgrade, Yugoslavia, the Sunday after Wimbledon. Because the women's final was switched to Sunday, the exhibition was rescheduled for Monday.

After numerous discussions, the promoter of the exhibition agreed to rent a Lear jet for us to fly from London to Belgrade. Willard, Patrick, and Al and Velma Nellum accompanied me on what can only be described as a maddening, three-day venture. We flew from London to Belgrade to Frankfurt, Germany, then Wurzburg, Germany, before heading home to Houston.

We were met in Terminal I at London's Heathrow Airport by a man who hauled all of our baggage. That, by the way, was no small feat since I had been in Europe for almost a month. Another man led us to a bus that took us directly to the plane. Less than fifteen minutes passed between the time we parked and the time we entered the plane, hardly the norm when taking international flights. The pilots were already on board, and the engines were running.

They were obviously much more eager to be airborne than I was. Yes, count me among those who see nothing exciting about flying through what United Airlines calls the friendly skies. Though my chosen career requires me to zip through floating clouds quite frequently, I would prefer not to fly. Especially in those small props.

Once—earlier in my career—when I was scheduled to fly to Tokyo, I dreamed that the plane was going to be full of snakes. I was frantic. Mama got a Pan Am pilot friend of hers to calm me down. I did make the flight, but I was scared to death the whole way. I don't like roller coasters, either. Don't put me on anything that can cause motion sickness.

I haven't been quite as fearful of flying in recent years, mainly because I've just put my trust in the Lord. If my final moments of life on Earth are going to be spent in a downward spiral on an airplane, then so be it. Planes don't scare me as much because my faith is stronger.

Thankfully, my apprehensions about flying a Lear jet from London to Belgrade were unfounded. It was a relaxing trip. I slept like a baby all the way to Belgrade. We arrived shortly after one o'clock Monday morning, a bit exhausted but excited nonetheless. After being whisked through customs, we went directly to the Marriott hotel, which was located in the middle of downtown Belgrade.

The former Yugoslavia's capital—population about one million— is flanked by two rivers, the Danube and the Sava. It's one of those ancient European cities that was established before Jesus walked the Earth. It reminds me of Paris, primarily because its wide boulevards are also lined with trees, mostly chestnuts. Everything there seemed green and alive.

Later that morning, Monica and I held a press conference in what seemed to be Belgrade's city hall. A translator helped me through the questioning. Afterwards, I spoke with Belgrade Mayor Unkovich in his private office. When I think about that meeting, I often wonder if he had any idea that in two years, his country would be torn apart by one of the bloodiest civil wars in recent history.

We ate lunch at the hotel, then set off for practice. The red clay surface was quite different from the grass I had played on the last three weeks. The muscles used to set up to hit a ball on clay are different from those used on grass. On clay courts you're hitting everything high; on grass courts you're hitting everything low. You're using your thighs and butt muscles because you're having to do more in the squat position.

My biggest concern was injuring myself during the exhibition. Exhibitions afforded me an opportunity to earn a hefty paycheck while pleasing many fans who wanted to see me play. But it's not a time to fight for every point. You try to be competitive, but that's not always possible because you know—win or lose—your computer ranking won't be affected. Injuries seem to occur often during exhibitions, probably because players think more about the possibility of getting hurt than they do about moving freely and agilely. I know I did, especially on the heels of reaching the Wimbledon final. A number of promotional appearances, other exhibitions, media events, and tour stops were scheduled for the rest of the year. This would not be a good time to come up lame.

I did manage to honor all of my commitments that year. Not wanting people to say that my Wimbledon success had changed me probably helped me stay on track. But keeping those commitments wore me out physically and probably cost me more in the long run than anyone realized.

Even before Monica turned pro, one look at her smacking a tennis ball was enough to convince you that she would be special. She had that nobody-can-beat-me look in her eye from the first time I saw her. You don't know when a person with that look is going to hit the big time; you just know they're going to hit it.

Monica got her revenge in that match, which was played at about 5:30 P.M. in front of an expected partisan crowd. She won in straight sets. My goal was to give the fans a good show and have some fun. Judging by the reaction, I'm pretty sure my mission was accomplished.

That evening, the promoters held a dinner in honor of Monica and me. Monica and her family had left Yugoslavia to live in Florida a few years earlier, so the dinner was a big homecoming.

That Wednesday, we flew to Frankfurt, Germany, where we were met by Olaf Merkel, the promotions manager for S. Oliver. He was our guide for the next thirty-six hours. As we crossed the Frankfurt Airport, numerous autograph seekers and well-wishers slowed our trek. I felt like doing a Sally Field impression, screaming, "You love me; you really love me," but decided the humor might get lost in the translation.

Besides, I was truly touched when I remembered that I had beaten Graf, Germany's revered superstar, in the Wimbledon semifinals. The airport fans didn't seem to care about that, which made me feel like a world celebrity.

We spent our first day in Germany on a shopping spree at Hugo Boss' main factory, which is located just outside Stuttgart. Many of the top men and women players of my era favored the Boss line. Clothing factory officials periodically arranged for players and their guests to visit the factory. They offer the players discounts on top-of-the-line clothing and, believe me, their merchandise is too good to resist. Patrick had talked to Christophy Rossenauer, Hugo Boss' promotions manager, to allow us to make a special visit. As I said earlier, and will say again and again, being a Wimbledon finalist definitely made me feel special.

After filling several Hugo Boss travel bags with suits, shirts, socks, ties, and other items, we headed for the tiny village of Wurzburg. Nestled in a valley, Wurzburg is situated in the southern part of Germany. In the background, I could see a castle perched on a hill. We were told that wine grapes were grown on the side of the hill. Later, we learned that grapes from the village were pretty potent. That leads to a funny story. Be patient; I'll tell you about it.

My Wimbledon deal with S. Oliver required me to make an appearance at the company's headquarters in Wurzburg. That evening we had dinner with S. Oliver's chairman, Bernd Frier, and his family.

My understanding was that Frier had started small, but soon became the CEO of one of the largest jean and casual clothing businesses in Germany. Frier knew that Germans were crazy about tennis because of Boris and Steffi, but I think he liked me because I was an underdog who made good. He probably figured that we had traveled similar paths to success. I was a poor black who struggled to survive in a predominantly white sport; he was a small-business guy who hung in there and survived against Germany's clothing manufacturing giants.

I should have a place in the Guinness Book of Records for being the guest of honor at—in terms of distance—the most wide-ranging dinner parties in the shortest time period. Including my Wimbledon celebration dinner Saturday night at Fontana di Trevi, the German bash was my third party in five days in three different countries. But I was okay; the adrenaline was still flowing.

Our German hosts spoke fluent English. Among other things, we discussed tennis and blue jeans. Here's the funny part about the hillside grapes. Our hosts warned us not to drink too much because the alcohol content of their wine, made from those grapes, is higher than that of American wine.

I only had a taste—to be polite—but Willard and Patrick kept trying to keep pace with our hosts. After enjoying a glass of wine or two too many, Willard and Patrick were nearly three-sheets-to-the-wind drunk. Before our dessert was served, Patrick advised Willard that it was customary for one of the guests to offer a toast. Willard stood up but had a tough time stringing coherent sentences together. He mumbled a while longer; then we urged him to take a seat.

The wine of Wurzburg had made its point. Our new German friends thought Willard was quite funny, as did Patrick, who frequently reminded Willard of his garbled toast when we got back home.

The next morning, I made an appearance at S. Oliver's main store in Wurzburg. Even though they had only one day to promote the

*My friends, the AA tennis players from Wimbledon: each year we got together to see a play in London. I did this for about 12 years, from 1985 until I retired in 1997.*

event, before I arrived a long line had formed outside the store. I signed autographs inside for several hours. I was surprised but pleased that so many people came to meet me during my short stay in that quaint little German town.

Afterwards, store officials invited us to browse and collect whatever we wanted. Each of us left the store with two large trash bags full of clothing. As we checked out, the lady helping us looked disappointed. She wondered if we liked their clothing because she didn't think we had taken enough. We all laughed, unable to believe their generosity. I still have some of the sweaters and jeans that I picked up from S. Oliver's. I knew the security guards in U.S. Customs were going to be very interested in speaking to us upon our arrival.

I got one other blockbuster treat before leaving Germany: a telephone call from then-President George Bush. He wanted us to be his guests at a Republican function that was to be held in Houston.

That was just too much. We were making jokes, telling each other that we'd only go if Air Force One came to pick us up.

I had been on airplanes so often I didn't know which way was up anymore. When I finally did return home, nearly everyone in the media wanted to interview me. I appeared on the Arsenio Hall Show later that year and was involved in more off-the-court stuff than you can imagine.

It was fun while it lasted, but there was a down side. Too much time away from the court caused my game to slip. I wasn't as sharp on the court the rest of the year, and loss after loss got me depressed. I knew I should have taken more time for myself and gotten some rest. Later, Patrick agreed that my schedule and the demands on me that year hurt my performance. All that traveling and doing other things besides the things that got me to Wimbledon in the first place took a toll. I was exhausted, and before I knew it, I was in a bad drought. It was a valuable lesson.

Do I look back in regret when I think of what might have been? Not really. I'm comfortable with the routes I chose, even though some roads have been far rougher and more painful than I dreamed possible. I believe something called destiny has much to do with what I did and what I didn't do. For the most part, the good things tend to balance out the bad things during the course of a lifetime. Only the truly lucky ones have smooth sailing all the time.

# 16

## Love Slips Away

I FIND IT DIFFICULT to believe that I will forever be burdened with bulimia, an illness that more often afflicts young white women. I also never believed I would fall under a dark cloud of depression. I like to think I am a basically high-energy, sunny person but, in the spring of 1999, the heartaches associated with my daily life got to be too much to bear. I saw no hope of securing the family life I've always yearned to have. And, on top of that, may faith had become shaky. My spirit suddenly wasn't there.

I tried to ease the pain by binging and purging but, in early May, a telephone call from Willard made me experience a depth of sadness I didn't know existed on this Earth. No matter what I told myself, it just wouldn't go away.

What was "it"?

Basically, not being able to sleep, not being able to concentrate for longer than five minutes at most, mind constantly wondering, 'What will become of me? Where will I go? Will I ever get out of this?'

I stayed in bed. I has no motivation to do anything. When people asked me out, I was always, always, always making excuses for why I couldn't do this or that. I'm very close to my family; yet I didn't want to see any of them either. I just wanted to be in a corner, by myself, with nobody around. Even being the champion at heart I feel I am, I couldn't get myself to do the simplest act. I could only focus on what had happened to me in the past. I was no longer a tennis player; I was no longer married; I was no longer young; I was no longer special. My moment had passed. It was as though I had never played tennis at all. I was a total failure.

I was also negative to people, and you know that's not me. I couldn't get a positive out of anything. When people tried to be friendly, I was negative back. All the time I was thinking, 'What are you going to do to me? What do you want?'

For three months I hid.

I lived in darkness. It was like major thunderstorms; the whole world was pitch black, only inside me, and it kept rolling in, and it never ended. I felt sad and gloomy. There wasn't light anymore.

In this kind of low state, when I tried to move my feet, I felt the world was directly on top of me. I never knew life could feel that heavy. Put this together with bulimia, and I was playing a doubles match solo against two of God's toughest opponents. I didn't want to admit I was in over my head, but I was. They had the court covered from end to end, back to front. There was nowhere I could put the ball.

If someone had drawn a picture of me then, they would have had to have put a cloud over my head. It was that obvious. Wherever I went, I brought the cloud with me. People would say, "Smile; life isn't that bad." People I didn't know on the street would turn to me: "You need to smile, girl." Strangers. I always thought I felt okay or, if I didn't, I looked okay. I checked out mirrors to make sure I was still normal; I didn't think it showed. But people see your inner soul and feel your inner turmoil; they know there's a dark cloud over you.

The binging and purging had caused a serious chemical imbalance in my blood system. At times, the world had seemed like it was spinning a hundred miles per hour. Now I know why.

John Lucas was the one who got me to see that I needed help and couldn't do it alone. John was not only a two-sports star (basketball and tennis), but an outspoken drug user who changed his life and the lives of many others in the NBA as well as other sports. He made me realize that I must first want help to save myself, and that the request was going to have to come from within me. He also personally made sure that I had space and time to get the help I needed. He was a true angel who came into my life at the right time.

I attended therapy sessions every day while I was hospitalized. Much of the time I sat between a next to stockbroker and crack addict, who kept saying that he was just waiting to get out so he could get another hit. At that moment I realized that anybody from any walk of life could be sitting next to me. We're all human beings, all basically the same. No matter how successful a person seems from the outside, he or she usually has a private struggle of some kind. We're all working on something. The therapy kind of brought me back to reality and convinced me that I could fight through any problem, overcome any burden, survive any heartbreak, including my dysfunctional relationship with Willard. But I'm not sure I could have gotten myself together without the help John gave me.

After all that I had achieved with Willard, after all that we had gone through, I wanted to believe that my marriage would last forever. Given the odds, I guess I should be grateful that we stayed together for six years. Our marriage ended in the fall of 1997. Incompatibility was the reason he gave in the divorce petition. I'm still trying to move on, trying not to harbor any bad feelings toward Willard. But I do. It irritates me to hear his name. Maybe in time it won't matter.

Before Willard, I dated Richard Johnson, a former Houston Oilers cornerback. That was an experience too. I realized then what it was like to care about somebody who really didn't care about me. Richard had his own agenda.

We dated on and off for three years. Actually, he always decided when we should get together. Once when Richard got me a ticket to an Oilers' home game, I sat next to another black woman, who I later learned was also dating Richard. Apparently, Richard knew where we were sitting. Occasionally he'd wave. The woman sitting next to me and I waved back. After the game, he gave that same woman an affectionate bear hug. I was crushed for days. I will always care about Richard. But then one day in the fall of 1988, Willard, speaking his syrupy Texas drawl, walked into my life.

I met Willard through Edgar Harvey, a family friend. My sister Clara couldn't pick me up from the airport one day, so she asked Edgar to get me. He wanted to stop by his office before dropping me at my hair salon. When we got to his office, he asked me to come in to meet his partner.

I was thinking his partner was going to be an old man with a big belly hanging over his belt. I had on a T-shirt, sweat pants, and my hair wasn't combed at all. When we walked into the office, Willard's back was facing us. When he turned around, I spoke to him quickly, then ran out the door. I thought he was so good-looking, and I was too shy to try to get to know him right away.

When I arrived at the salon, one of the hair stylists was showing photos taken at a recent party. NBA players Spud Webb and Dominique Wilkins and several entertainers were among the celebrities in the photos. I told her and the others about this guy I had just met. I described Willard, but nobody could place him. I was under the dryer when Willard himself walked in. Surprise, surprise! He handed me a business card, saying it would help me to remember his name. I thought, 'How arrogant!'

After Willard left, I asked again if anybody knew who he was. Turns out, quite a few people did, but nobody knew him by that name. On the social scene he was "Blade." There were even several pictures of Willard with Spud in the photo album.

That same day Willard called me on his car phone. It didn't take long for us to get starry-eyed over each other. About two months after we met—and just a few days before I left for the 1988 Australian Open—he proposed. I broke the news to Willis, my coach at the time, when I saw him at the Australian Open. Willis asked me if I was sure that I wanted to get married in the middle of my career. I said yes. I told Willis his name, but he'd never heard of him.

I think I liked Willard mainly because he seemed so self-assured. He was always very positive about life, goal-oriented. I knew he was arrogant, but hey, I like arrogant men. I believe that any man who doesn't have at least a touch of arrogance might feel uneasy in my world. Probably more so when I was among the top players in the world.

Being in the limelight can be an uncomfortable—at times troubling—experience for a companion. Case in point: Though I changed my name to Zina Garrison-Jackson, most people still called me Zina Garrison. The most embarrassing moments for me came when someone would say to Willard, "Oh, Mr. Garrison, how are you?" I ached for Willard when that happened. I've seen it happen to other celebrities and their spouses. Yet it wasn't the end of the world; I often felt like telling my husband, "Get a grip, idiot!"

When I returned from Australia, Willard met me in Washington, D.C., and confessed that he had changed his mind. He called our engagement off. I got mad and felt crushed, and I started crying. Then he pulled out a ring and said he was just kidding. Again, he asked me to marry him and again I said yes.

I had asked Willard to meet me in Washington because I wanted him to meet Al and Velma Nellum, my surrogate parents, who lived in Reston, Virginia. Al played the typical father role quite well. He cross-examined Willard, speaking in a firm 'Boy, what-are-your-intentions' tone.

Here's how Al and Velma recalled the day I brought Willard "home" to meet them.

Velma: "We spent a couple of days getting to know him. She was very happy about us meeting him, and we knew she wanted very much for us to like him."

Al: "I think we both felt that we needed to be her parents through this. When the marriage was set, I said, 'Let's talk about finances' because we wanted to help her. We agreed to pay for the reception.

As it turned out, the reception cost more than most weddings. She was very, very happy and it was good to see her happy."

In the beginning my family in Houston thought it was too soon, that I was rebounding from Richard, and that I wasn't really thinking this out. But I had a good feeling about Willard.

I discussed my feelings for Willard with Dewayne Flowers, a good friend, who was also Richard's best friend. He said that if I really loved Willard then I should go with it and not worry about what people might think. He helped me understand that I had to follow my heart and not what everybody else was telling me.

We were married September 23, 1989.

Though some family members questioned the wisdom of my decision, everyone helped shape my wedding-day activities, which if I must say so myself, became one of Houston's most talked-about black social events of 1989. Everyone got involved, and I absolutely did nothing. I did choose my wedding gown. My sisters, my aunts, and Willard's mom and sister accompanied me on this special shopping expedition. I don't know how many dresses I considered, but the very first one I tried on was the one I chose. My aunts thought the dress was cut too low in both the back and front. However, since I was paying for it, I was getting what I wanted.

My twin sisters handled the flower arrangements—appropriately, because that's how they earn their living. I chose non-relatives to coordinate the wedding because I wanted less pressure from the family. I had twelve bridesmaids and twelve ushers. Robin Givens, Lori McNeil, Katrina Adams, Kim Davis, and Sheryl Woods were among my bridesmaids.

I had two maids of honor—Leola and Lisa Lane. From the start, Lisa and her sister decided they didn't like Willard. They said he was a gold-digger. Lisa did everything she could to ruin the wedding. She had me crying the day we had our reception party. I don't know why my eyes weren't all puffy on my wedding day because I actually had been up all night crying. Lisa kept saying I was only marrying Willard because Richard wasn't there for me.

My bridal shower was held at Lisa's mother's house. Someone told me Richard was there, but I never saw him. We all got high on tequila. One of my friends split her toe, so we crowded into the limo and rushed her to this little hospital on the west side.

Too much tequila caused us to be a bit too raunchy at the hospital. Several hospital employees requested us to keep the noise down. We told them off. The tequila made us do that, too. The limousine driver told me to get out of there because they had called the police. The cops arrived just as we were leaving. I sometimes wonder if we would have been put in jail overnight had we stayed at the hospital. That would have been an awful way to start a new life. I'm just glad we got out of there in time.

Surprisingly, everything went pretty smoothly on my wedding day. Rodney and my Uncle Morris gave me away. All the way down the aisle, Rodney kept saying, "Are you sure you want to do this? We can turn back any time now." The preachers were laughing hysterically.

I'm thinking to myself, 'I can't believe he's saying this.' My uncle told Rodney to leave me alone.

I had twelve bridesmaids passing tissues down the line. My friend Kim Davis was bawling. We went to the reception at the Ritz-Carlton in a rented 1957 Rolls Royce. Supposedly there were only two in the world at the time, and one of them was in Houston. Traffic was stopped on 610; I felt like the President—no one on the freeway but the Rolls and twelve limos.

I had never been to a reception where everyone had a camera. We must have posed for hours. Finally, we made it to the cake. Then there were more pictures. I don't even remember dancing.

Willard and I looked at each other at about the same time and said, "Let's go." We went up to our room, ordered room service, took a bite out of our hamburgers, and fell asleep.

I was disappointed when I learned that John Wilkerson didn't come to my wedding. I think his absence symbolically signaled the end of my dependence on him. Perhaps I felt that I needed to get married in order to take another step in my life and to be comfortable with myself. Willard's charm and self-confidence were characteristics I admired. I hoped to be as outgoing as he was.

We didn't have a honeymoon because I had to leave for Tokyo a couple of days later to play in a Federation Cup match. The following week, I played in an exhibition match in Acapulco, so we honeymooned there. Our first year of marriage was spent traveling from tournament to tournament. I thought it was wonderful that Willard was willing to set aside his career plans to help me achieve my goals in tennis. We talked about that before we were married and agreed that the roles would be reversed later on.

I felt fortunate during that first year because Willard never criticized me after a loss. He was always very supportive. We had one big argument, which occurred a couple of weeks before the 1990 Wimbledon. In front of Sherwood of all people, Willard tried to talk to me about getting to the net. I exploded. "Don't tell me about tennis because I don't tell you how to run your business!"

I might have lingered on the subject a bit longer than I should have, but we understood that neither should interfere with the other's business. That incident occurred after I lost a match in Eastbourne. That was the only time Willard tried to be my coach.

Actually, Willard was a pretty good athlete. His sister, Cookie Craig, told me he was a hot-shot basketball star for Denton (Texas) High School. I watched him hit tennis balls a little bit while we were in Spain and was amazed at how much he had picked up just from watching and listening to the coaches.

The little squabble I had with Willard at Eastbourne motivated me to work harder during my preparation for the '90 Wimbledon. We arrived there with a clear understanding of what we expected from each other and what we had to do.

Willard was a reliable help-mate at Wimbledon, but during my last few years on tour, it was a battle to get him to travel with me. He always said he had to work or he was too tired. By 1995, I was ready to retire and start a family, but he thought I should stay on tour and earn more money. It bothered me that he wanted me to keep playing but didn't want to travel with me. He was frequently mentally abusive during that time, too. He called me lazy, ugly, and a lot of other unflattering things. He also had started seeing other women. I couldn't believe it when I learned that he was having an affair with one of my best friends. At least, I thought she was one of my best friends.

Evidently, Willard had flings even when we were traveling together. One time, when I was playing Conchita Martinez at the U.S. Open, Willard gave one of my friends a wad of cash in the grandstand to rent a limousine to pick up his girlfriend at the airport. He also got her a room at the Plaza Hotel and the whole nine yards. He did all that while I was out there on the court playing a match, earning money for us! How can a person do that? Did I deserve that kind of disrespect?

As painful as my experiences with Willard and other black men have been, I know I'm not the only well-to-do black woman who has had a troublesome relationship with a black man. A woman worth more than her spouse generally finds a bucket full of heartache. Money does make a difference. It's undoubtedly difficult for any independent, highly successful woman of any color to find a man who won't develop an ego problem when his spouse or companion makes more money than he does.

Women's liberation made it possible for many women to be their family's major breadwinner. So, all you chauvinist men out there, wake up and get over it! It's a new day as well as a new millennium.

Some men have handled the change better than others. From my perspective, it seems that black men have a tougher time accepting black women as equal partners. Even strong black men have a tendency to shy away from wealthy black women because they're not able to accept the reversal of roles. I can't understand why most black men in my income bracket allow their egos to get in the way of forming a loving bond with a strong black woman. The fact that I can support myself ought to be a positive.

Many black male athletes say they marry white women because they know a white woman isn't going to be arguing all the time. Does that mean they'd prefer to have someone who's going to sit there and be a doormat just to get their money over someone who's going to love them and challenge them to be a better person?

I'll never understand why a man wouldn't want a mate who's capable of making a substantial financial contribution to the family. It's no wonder so many successful black women seek happiness with white men. What else can they do?

I don't go that way myself. Nothing against white people, but I just like the brothers. I like the strength and dominance that I feel a black man projects. Unfortunately, the only strong black women that most black men seem capable of cherishing are their moms.

I have a very good friend who's married to a white guy. He's a very nice white guy, and that's her choice. I think they are compatible. It's possible to fall in love with a person of a different race but, for some reason, white strippers seem to be the women of choice for a lot of black male athletes. That's happening more than you think. I just don't get it.

Some black athletes spend so much of their money at these strip tease joints it's not even funny. Look at former NBA superstar Charles Barkley. He said he loved Houston because we have some of the best strip joints. He spoke those words on nationwide TV! It's very interesting that as soon as black male athletes start making those big salaries, white women are all over them at nightclubs. Black women stand in the corner watching. I am not saying that white women weren't attracted to them before; I'm just saying it's pretty clear why they are attracted to them now.

I also don't get Dennis Rodman saying he doesn't want to have anything to do with sisters because they weren't attracted to him in high school. So what? A lot of people looked like ugly ducklings in high school. He's still using that as an excuse and he's in his thirties?

Of course, you also have the situation where some high-profile black women are going to white men because they've been mistreated by black men. I think in either direction, whether it's black men with white women or black women with white men, problems can occur when these people look for happiness in the wrong place. It's inside. It's finding the love within yourself or love with God.

Sometimes God takes you to places and takes things away from you to get you back on track to return to Him. That's how we find true peace and happiness. If you put your faith in flesh, pain and fear will always follow you.

At times, my heart aches for the life I used to have and the family life I was looking forward to having. The toughest moments come when I see my girlfriends with their kids, shopping, going to McDonald's....

I know bulimia will continue to be a scar in my throat. It'll stay inactive as long as I don't pick at the scab with my finger.

I believe in love and still want to get married and raise a family. I very much want to have a baby. I have faith that it will happen. Only through my strong faith did I survive what I now realize was an abusive marriage. With the Lord's guidance, I'll find a way to stay strong, move on, and become a better person.

# 17

# Just Zina

'M HUMBLED by the special attention I receive from fans throughout the world. I feel truly honored when both working-class and corporate-type people I've never seen ask for my autograph, give me gifts, and do favors for me. I used to think that it was strange for people to want my autograph, especially when they'd ask me to write it on a napkin or any piece of paper they could find. But as I got older, I realized that there were several people that had become very special to me in the same way. I still hope to meet Nelson Mandela and Bishop Desmond Tutu. If I ever do, I wouldn't hesitate to ask for their autographs.

I consider Motown's Berry Gordy the most impressive person I've known. In the 1960s, every singer who was a star in the record business became a megastar when they joined Motown. He manufactured legends.

I feel truly blessed to be able to call Maya Angelou a friend. She's the wisest of grandmothers and soul-mothers, always coming up with the perfect phrase, the perfect word. She has always been so comforting. When I first met her, I didn't say a word the whole time. I just stared in awe. Later, when she invited me to her house for dinner, I talked her head off. Every Thanksgiving she cooks dinner for a group of friends, and I try to join them.

Being a celebrity *is* kind of cool. Makes you feel special. There have been times when I'd spend hours practicing writing my name so it would look distinctive, just right. One day Katrina said, "Why write your whole name? There's only one Zina."

I said, "You've got a point." Now I sign just Zina. Short, sweet, and to the point. In a way, it sums up me as a personality. Nothing fancy. Just Zina.

The autograph thing has gotten so big and there's so much money to be made that it's being abused. I don't think athletes should be requesting money for their autographs. The public has made it possible for us to have so much. Why can't we give them something back, free of charge? For the most part, we earn a good living and are treated special. Which raises another question.

Why is it that so many people rarely hesitate to do things for famous people, but they usually complain about doing things for our country's truly needy?

Don't get me wrong. It's nice to be put on a pedestal with other professional athletes. I just think it would be so much better if more of us, particularly celebrities, politicians, and corporate types, would do more for those who are not as popular but genuinely need assistance. Greed is a terrible thing to promote, but that's what we do all the time. What would the world be like if athletes, actors, actresses, pop stars, and other public figures routinely practiced generosity and compassion? Just think how differently children and teens would behave if they saw their idols working for humanity and disadvantaged people rather than just for themselves. Imagine what it would be like to have role models expressing charitable and humanitarian rather than materialistic and "me-first" values.

It's one thing to wear your religion on your sleeve; it's another to act as God's true servant. And that means having an open heart, not just quoting Bible verses and sectarian rules.

Many of us could be doing better jobs as parents, too. Something's dreadfully wrong with the way children are being raised these days. I blame their parents, who seem to have an uncontrollable need to give their kids everything they want. That's one reason why we're experiencing a breakdown in the family structure.

Too many kids—blacks and whites—are getting too much too soon. The only thing they seem to respect is the value of the gifts they receive, never the person giving the gifts. If you buy them a pair of Reebok tennis shoes when Nikes are the footwear of the moment worn by the in crowd, then Reeboks won't do: "Take 'em back!"

The next year, if Reebok becomes hot and you bring home the same Nikes, they look at you as if you're nuts.

What are we teaching our children? Do we really believe they should be slaves of marketing fashion? Do we want to reinforce the idea that that's normal, that that's even sane? Where are our values?

I watch my sister Clara with her younger daughter, Yolanda. Clara let her go out to the skating rink at 11 o'clock one night! This kid also has a weekend planner and gets her nails done regularly! I ask, Why? When do we reclaim control of our kids and not let them control us?

It's sad that so many parents, including Clara, have this give-'em-anything-they-want child-rearing attitude. They seem to think their children will rebel if they don't give in to their every whim. I'm surprised that Clara isn't more of a disciplinarian. I know mama and Granny were as strict with her as they were with me.

I don't remember ever being told directly, but when I was a kid, family gatherings were mandatory. They were also very special. After going to church on Sunday, we always ate dinner as a family, just like they did in the movie *Soul Food*.

We talked about our activities—in school and in the community—our needs, dislikes, and dreams. I shared both the silliness and intimacies of my life with mama. Looking back, I realize that my daily interaction with family and friends helped me develop a moral barometer which, to this day, shapes my attitude about right and wrong. I believe those family gatherings made me the giving person that I am.

Though the visions that I experienced as a child were very strong,

I stopped having them as I got older. Still, there are times when I feel compelled to act on ideas and thoughts that shoot into my mind out of the blue.

Katrina Adams is among a handful of people I've told about the visions I had when I was a kid. She gets very nervous when I tell her about these gut feelings that occasionally come over me. Recalling one such incident, Katrina told this story: "In 1988, Zina and I were on a plane to Japan after the Virginia Slims Championships when she had a vision or insight about wanting to start this homeless program. We had formed a close, trusting friendship and she unhesitatingly showed me a side that few people see. I encouraged her to follow her feelings and find out what had to be done. She did just that and within a year, the Zina Garrison Foundation for the Homeless opened in Houston."

Some people, especially those in the media, want to believe that I am a typical poor little black girl from Texas who made good. That's not the way I see myself. I lived in a decent neighborhood, had plenty of food, and never went to school without lunch money. I was spoiled and had everything I wanted. How can I say I was poor?

However, I do know what it means to be poor and without hope. I share the pain of the downtrodden who struggle every day to make ends meet. Most people are so far removed from the black subculture that it's tough for them to fathom the day-to-day problems of the working-class poor, most of whom live in the inner cities.

There are so many children—black and white—growing up in homes without fathers or caring father figures. A man who fathers a child then ducks out on his parental responsibilities is a wimp. Too many black men are acting like wimps. They have all these kids and they don't take care of them. Women who allow this to happen have no self-respect. Teen pregnancy is a problem that is not confined to the black community. I read somewhere that more and more eighth- and ninth-grade white girls are getting pregnant. Kids that age have a tough enough time dealing with the usual teenage problems. It's easy to understand how it could be a nightmare for anyone that young to be burdened with raising a child. It angers me to see so many men, black and white, going about their business with no concern for their children or the mothers of their children.

Divorce laws have made it easier for men to walk away from their parental obligations. It's so easy for them to say, 'It's not going to work, let me out.' I could go on and on about that.

There are so many homes where family members abuse drugs or alcohol. Women burdened by poverty and multiple children often lose respect for themselves. When kids sense that you have no respect for yourself, then they are not going to respect you, either.

To me, that explains why the message that so many rap artists are sending out in their music is so nasty and anti-woman. I'm for playing hard and taking no prisoners; my game spoke for itself—but listen to the words of some of these songs. They're not about playing hard or fair. They're about being mean, about feeling important by degrading others. I'd like to see some of those tough guys try walking around Sierra Leone where the locals "rap" by cutting off hands.

I don't think nastiness is tough. A real warrior knows how to disarm and embrace his wounded brothers and sisters. He doesn't just add to the woundedness of the community.

Willard listened to rap a lot when we were together. Often, after I sat in the car with him listening to rap, I got the feeling that I wanted to fight somebody and I didn't know why. I didn't really pay that much attention to the lyrics, but I must have gotten the message. I have nieces and nephews who listen to that stuff, and they look like the world is about to fall in on them all the time. I had no idea that a "gat" is a gun or a "grio" is your whole mouth filled with gold. Rap is a world tainted with self-loathing, violence, and negative vibes.

When I look at what's happening in the job market, I see a mean world getting meaner. "Downsizing" by major corporations is creating an even larger pool of unemployed and desperate folks. The loss of welfare checks by many single moms is making life especially tough for folks with nowhere to go.

Some experts predict that, because of the 1996 welfare law (which places a five-year limit on cash benefits and requires most recipients to find work within two years), more than one million children will live in poverty.

Actually, because it removed a lot of undeserving people from the system, the law reform was a positive step. I do, however, think the government could have devised a more gradual remedy. People act as though the majority of the folks on welfare are black, but that's not true. More than half are white. It's irritating to me when I look at a story about welfare on television and all you see are black faces.

I am waiting for the day when I'll see more black faces on the men's and women's tennis tours rather than on welfare lines. I'll probably have a good long wait. Today's youngsters don't seem to have the same commitment to the game that Lori and I had. It's definitely a different era.

When I was a kid, I couldn't wait to go outside to play with my friends. We'd spend hours at playgrounds, creating games and exploring the outdoors and the wonderful world of animal and bug life. Today's youngsters, depending on their neighborhood, have other choices. Many city kids are busy dodging stray bullets, trying to learn in substandard schools, and saying (hopefully) no to drug dealers and pimps. The youthful suburbanites in middle America spend hours of leisure time at shopping malls or surfing the net. What a choice! The real world is dangerous, with adults out of control and kids in gangs, and the virtual world is artificial and turns people into robots.

Our children are being seduced by the dark side of computers, and we don't seem to care. Kids don't have to go outside to enjoy themselves anymore. The games they play are ready-made and, with a handy computer mouse, only a click or two away. Computers are marvelous inventions and great learning tools, but I hope we don't allow them to deprive our children of wholesome and invigorating adventures that only can be experienced while interacting with friends and playmates in a real environment. We have flesh-and-blood bodies that are alive and need to feel themselves, to play and compete.

Kids who are active and happy in the outdoors, whether through sports or hiking or farming, don't engage in Goth cults or hatch dark schemes about how to revenge themselves on their classmates. I know many imaginative games are available on computers, but a youngster's imagination needs the challenge of competitive sports and real-life experiences, too—good and bad—to be fully developed. We are not cartoon characters, and it is a shame that we try to squeeze ourselves down into little screens.

That's one of the reasons the Zina Garrison All-Court Tennis Program was launched in the summer of 1992. It took two years to work through the bureaucracy and raise the money to make the program a reality. It's a year-round operation, with kids participating at several Houston parks, including MacGregor and Memorial. Now in its seventh year, the program has seen 6,000 youngsters participate. There's no charge to the kids. The USTA (United States Tennis Association) has provided a grant to the Academy for the last three years. The funding from the USTA comes from the Players Development Program for inner city and minority youth. This is exactly what the Academy is all about.

John and I dreamed and talked about creating this academy for many years. We saw that we couldn't rely on Texas tennis officials to do what was necessary to get more minorities exposed to tennis. We felt it was part of our responsibility to pave the way for disadvantaged kids to get the training needed to pursue pro careers.

While John and I can take credit for coming up with the idea, Willard made the contacts and had the savvy to make it happen. He went to his politically connected friends for support and made friends with other movers. Former mayor Bob Lanier, Sheila Jackson Lee, Karin Barth, Russell Bowers, Jack Blanton and his son Eddie are among our main supporters. Rodney Harmon, who is Director of Multicultural Player Development for the USTA, has been instrumental in helping implement programs for African-American youngsters around the country. He has also been a great help for the program.

I am very proud of this program.

I'm not an aggressive person by nature, but that's what's needed if we're going to get the funds required every year. If I personally asked them to do it, people would probably give something to support the kids. I'm just not good at asking. I have the connections because of who I am, but I don't feel comfortable using them. I know I need to be a more assertive fund-raiser if the program is going to survive. The Academy's goal for 2001 is to complete a 7½ million dollar fund raising campaign. The funding would be used to build a major tennis center for Houston's youth, twelve minutes from downtown Houston.

Some of the kids have been in the tennis program since it began, and I've gotten to know them quite well. I like to go out to the courts and just hang out with them, say "hi," and see what's up. Now that I've retired I can spend more time with them. I get a great feeling when I watch a kid progress from not being able to hit a ball across the net on his first day to the point where he's beating everyone else. We've had some kids qualify to play in USTA national events. A few of our younger ones are the dominant players in their age group.

My own program reminds me of John's, the one in which my own tennis life began. I enjoy the continuity between my childhood and present life so much. I try to encourage everyone, especially young black women, to play tennis because you can learn so much about yourself: How well can I handle pressure situations? Am I too aggressive? Am I too careful? Am I a selfish doubles player? Am I in sync with my doubles partner?

Play tennis and you'll discover the answer to those questions and many others. You will also learn the tennis etiquette rules and other social graces. Tennis unquestionably helped me develop all the competitive, social, and business skills that I needed to survive and excel in the society at large.

I also hope to help young blacks, as well as young whites, appreciate and better understand the view of the world from a black person's perspective. Even successful African-Americans feel naturally uneasy in this culture. It doesn't matter who you are or what you've achieved. It was just as true for Althea Gibson and Arthur Ashe, for James Baldwin, Colin Powell, and Michael Jordan. In *Days of Grace,* Arthur said being black—not having AIDS—was "the great burden I've had to bear."

I understand precisely what Arthur was saying. Most black people do.

# 18

# Looking Ahead

T ISN'T EASY just to walk away from something you've done all your life. The closer I got to playing my final career match in 1995, the more I realized I wasn't quite ready to shut the door on that phase of my life. I started emphasizing the word *"might"* whenever the media posed any what-are-you-going-do-after-you-quit questions.

A long, heart-to-heart chat with Billie Jean King convinced me to extend my departure date. She told me that Martina Navratilova and Chris Evert had similar feelings when they first considered retirement, so I shouldn't feel foolish or abnormal for wanting to do battle with the young folks a while longer. She said any decision regarding my retirement date should come from within me, not someone else. I've always believed that my body would let me know when to stop, so it was good for me to hear Billie Jean say essentially the same thing.

Actually, after acknowledging publicly that I was postponing my retirement plans, I played pretty good tennis. But in the first few months of 1996, my body sent me several might-be-time-to-go messages. A shoulder injury dulled the sting of my groundstrokes, and my 32-year-old bones took longer to get in gear. I finished the year winning only one match in eight events.

I'm sure if Arthur had lived to see me play in '96 he would have known right away that my personal life was a mess. He always said that I carried my emotions on my sleeves. I guess anyone who watched me play could tell that my mind oftentimes was afloat in outer space, while my body was chasing tennis balls. To say I struggled through '96 would be putting it mildly. The fact that several younger, top-ranked pros left the tour that year was no consolation. Argentina's Gabriela Sabatini, Japan's Kimiko Date, and Bulgaria's Katerina Maleeva retired in 1996. Sabatini and Date were 26, and Maleeva was 27. While most people begin their professional careers in their mid-20s, most tennis pros are put out to pasture at my age or younger. Ever wonder why? A tennis career resembles the life-span of a Stone Age hunter among the glaciers.

To be a top player, you first must give up your childhood and make a total commitment long before you even think about joining the tour. Which means it wouldn't hurt if someone stuck a racket in your hand shortly after you stopped wearing diapers. If you're on course to be a top pro, you're apt to spend much of your pre-teen years training like a pro, traveling like a pro, and competing with all the other junior, wanna-be pros in the world. Most of the great champions—Andre Agassi, Bjørn Borg, Arthur Ashe, Steffi Graf, Chris Evert, Martina Navratilova—began preparing for pro careers before completing their first decade of life.

Guys don't like to hear this, but that old saying about girls developing at a faster rate than boys certainly seems to be true in tennis. Graf, Sabatini, Seles, and Martina Hingis are among many female top-ranked pros to win Grand Slam titles as teenagers. Yet Borg, Pete Sampras, and Michael Chang are among only a handful of the game's male teenaged Grand Slam champions.

Actually, women pros ruled in the late '90s, when several teens, including Hingis, Venus and Serena Williams, and Anna Kournikova, were among the game's major stars. People were intrigued by the mental toughness displayed by Hingis, dubbed the "Swiss miss" by the media. Many male fans admired the glamour of Kournikova, the blonde Russian baseliner. Others seemed in awe of the power displayed by the gifted African-American sisters, Venus and Serena. I've been fortunate to know and work with the Williams sisters, whose success has been phenomenal. Their mother and father did an excellent job as far as their tennis game *and* raising them as young ladies. And they have a lot more potential to fulfill.

The success of top-ranked teen pros undoubtedly will inspire other young girls to follow a similar path. Fame and fortune await the lucky ones, like Graf and Sabatini, who joined the pro tour at age 14 and managed to avoid burnout or career-ending injuries. However, several other top pros, including Tracy Austin, Andrea Jaeger, and Jennifer Capriati, were not so lucky.

Tracy, who won the U.S. Open in 1979 and 1981, left the tour in 1983 because of a back injury. She returned in 1994 but was forced to abandon her comeback after being injured in an automobile. Andrea, who reached the finals in the 1982 French Open and 1983 Wimbledon, had seven shoulder operations after she left the tour in 1985.

Jennifer, who was worth more than $6 million before she turned pro at 13, left the tour in a frazzle at age 17. She went through some real tough times, including arrests for shoplifting and possession of marijuana, and a couple of trips to drug rehab centers. Since 1996, Jennifer has made several comeback attempts. With the help of her father and Harold Solomon, who coached her for a year until the fall of 2000, Jennifer finally got on the right track. She reached the 2000 Australian Open semifinals—her best Grand Slam finish in nine years. A few weeks later, she jumped to No. 15 in the world, her highest ranking in six years.

Maybe years from now we'll be able to say that in January 2001, Jennifer bounced all the way back from being down-in-the-dumps with a remarkable victory Down Under. Considering her odyssey, it was truly heartwarming to see Jennifer capture her first Grand Slam title—the Australian Open—by defeating nemesis Monica Seles in the quarterfinals, No. 2 Lindsay Davenport in the semis, and top-ranked Martina Hingis in the final.

Go Jen-Jen Go! I pray that your troubles are behind you for good and that you'll be able to continue to stay clean and healthy and play great tennis.

When you think about what happened to Jennifer, Tracy, and Andrea, you wonder if it makes sense to expose young girls to such a demanding lifestyle before they truly understand what being a professional tennis player is all about. I support the Sanex WTA Tour's rule change that now requires female players to move more gradually toward a full-time pro career. At 14 years of development, I don't believe a female's body is ready for the physical and mental pounding it's likely to take on the pro tour. A 14-year-old just isn't equipped to take on that level of stress and responsibility, though some—and their parents dreaming of being rich—might kid themselves they are.

When you're on the tour, you're expected to act like a grownup, but basically you're still a child, with child-like needs and tendencies. The transition was rough for me, and I was 18 when I began my career. Now, just thinking about what to do with the rest of my life is a bit scary.

I know I'm not going to stray too far away from the game. I played the Virginia Slims Legends circuit in 1997–98. Martina Navratilova, Chrissie, Billie Jean, Tracy Austin, and Virginia Wade are among the former champions who competed for many years on the Slims tour. Philip Morris, the Slims' parent company, ended its sponsorship of women's tennis in 1994.

I think all women pros owe a special debt to Virginia Slims for helping start the tour and for being our major sponsor in the 1970s when no other corporation was interested. Virginia Slims did a great job as our tour sponsor and has continued to be a friend and major supporter of women's tennis.

Some people criticized us because the tour's major sponsor sold products that have proven to be hazardous to your health. But Virginia Slims officials never attempted to get any of the tour's athletes or administrators to promote cigarette smoking. I don't smoke, and most athletes I know don't smoke. I don't believe we should condemn the company that helped make it possible for so many women to become role models for young girls striving to become professional tennis players.

I have joined Chris, Martina, and other veterans of the WTA Tour in a venture that keeps us fit and in touch with fans of the game. We do several corporate outings, clinics, and exhibitions each year in cities throughout the country. Who says you have to quit living (or playing) after you retire?

I also talked to my friend Jamie Williams, a former NFL player, about how to approach retirement. He made the transition several years ago to the working world and had lots to say about it. Mary Joe Fernandez and I have talked about it a lot, too. Mary Joe married Tony Godsick, her agent, in the summer of 2000. She's looking forward to starting a family and a life apart from the tour.

People seem to think that most professional athletes, once they've tucked away their sneakers, can easily find a new career. Then too, a lot of people believe former pros don't need a job because they've made a ton of money. Because I made almost $5 million in prize money, everyone assumes I still have that money. I wish.

I spent a lot of money paying my coaches—John, Willis, Sherwood, Angel Lopez, and several others. Those guys were good, but they weren't cheap. For years, I didn't get the endorsement deals that provide the level of financial security everyone yearns to have. I've made some bad investments as well. Make no mistake about it, I'm taking and thinking about various jobs.

What might I have done with my life if I hadn't been a tennis player? I think about that all the time these days! I'd like to be my own version of Martha Stewart, maybe not as big as her enterprise, but I could be doing some crafty cooking and maybe have my own line of cookbooks! And something with communications, for sure. I love being in front of the camera. And whatever I do, I would hope to tie it in with helping people in some way.

In 1997–98, I worked as a reporter for HBO at Wimbledon. I

really loved being an analyst/commentator. I can put myself in the middle of a match as a coach as well as a former player and analyze what a competing player should or shouldn't do. A good analyst knows the strengths and weaknesses of the players involved and should be able to explain tactics and strategies to the viewers. A few years ago I talked to Chris Myers of ESPN about how to go about being an on-the-air performer. I told him that I am shy but understand that I have to be more gregarious, more assertive. I am totally different on-camera. I love the exposure!

I've also considered working for the USTA's junior development program because I have a desire to encourage more youngsters, especially inner-city blacks, to play tennis. But USTA politics probably would keep me from going in that direction.

For years, the USTA has talked about tapping the athletic talent that we all know can be found and is being squandered in our country's inner cities. Yet I can't understand why they have refused to hire people who know where to go and what to do. You can't place a country club pro in an inner-city environment and expect him or her to understand and appreciate the lifestyle of the inner-city kid. No matter how hard they try, they're not going to be able to relate.

As I've mentioned before, I was pretty puzzled by the USTA's refusal to seek out experienced black coaches, like John Wilkerson and Willis Thomas, when they first formed their junior development program in 1988. USTA presidents from Gordon Jorgensen (1988–90) to Les Snyder (1995–96) have talked about establishing programs to identify and train talented black kids, but nothing has been done. And because USTA officials have yet to consider hiring the two men who took these young black girls from a Houston public park to the top of the tennis world, I doubt if they'll ever do anything but talk.

For years, Arthur's was the only black voice that could stir action at the USTA. Dwight Mosely, the first black to sit on the USTA Board of Directors, didn't rock the boat much, though I know he occasionally helped USTA decision-makers understand the concerns of the black tennis community. Dwight was the USTA's secretary/trea-surer when he died in September 1996.

Still, I believe that input from a former top player of color might carry more weight with that group, and I suppose that's why I some-times wonder if I am destined to work with the USTA in some capac-ity. Like many blacks, I really don't want to believe that white America still has trouble treating me and people like me fairly. You can't help but think the worst when exceptional achievements by blacks in ten-nis are ignored.

For example, Houston city officials should have bent over back-wards to help John produce more top-ranked pros. Instead, they moved him out of MacGregor Park into an office job. What kind of sense does that make?

To get more minorities involved in tennis, we have to get out there in inner-city schools, parks, and recreational centers to let them know it's possible and to make them want to play. It's a tough assignment, though, no matter how you look at it. Once these kids reach a certain level they need money for coaching, they need facilities, they need to travel to events. It's an expensive sport and not economically feasible to get a lot of minorities to play. We're talking about $30,000 to $35,000 per kid per year just to get them on the level of a good college player.

Regardless of my career path, youngsters will forever be my spe-cial concern. That's why I'm working so hard to keep the Zina Gar-rison All-Court Tennis Program alive. When Lori and I gave our chats at MacGregor, we felt it was our responsibility to level with the kids. We told them that if they became good enough to be pros, they might be greeted by the same racial bias and hidden barriers that Lori and I still face. I guaranteed them they wouldn't last long if they acted like John McEnroe.

I still give talks at high schools throughout the country because I think it's important for youngsters everywhere to hear first-hand the thoughts of an African-American woman who made a living as a professional athlete. Yet I've cut back some on my high-school talks because I didn't really think people were listening. My nieces and

© K. Sachar

*With my nieces and nephews. I'm fourth from left.*

nephews say kids get tired of being preached to by athletes. They believe that athletes are more concerned about themselves than they are about what's going on in anyone else's life. Still, if I get just one or two kids to listen to me, I believe I will have done a good job.

Obviously, the best feeling for me is to know for sure that I've inspired, or helped in some small way, just one youngster to become a tennis pro. Hey, I might already have done that.

I remember hitting with two little sisters from Lafayette, Louisiana, who came to MacGregor Park during that time. Chanda Rubin was one of them. Her father, Ed, brought her along with her sister to meet Lori McNeil, John Wilkerson, and me. There still aren't that many African-Americans playing tennis, and they always have a way of seeking out the other ones for support or understanding of how to get through.

Chanda listened intently to everything that was said and executed the drills aggressively, like a little girl possessed. I've always liked and admired Chanda a lot. When she first turned pro, I knew I could find her in a corner of the players' lounge, reading a book.

Keep in mind that Chanda and golf phenom Tiger Woods had strong family support systems and didn't have to deal with the economic hurdles that most striving black athletes have had to negotiate. Chanda's father is a judge, and her mother, Bernadette, is a retired school teacher. Chanda grew up with a tennis court in her back yard. Tiger's father Earl, a retired Army officer, put a golf club in his son's hands before he could walk. In that sense, their experiences and opportunities were outside the norm of reality of most young black athletes.

I always felt it would be easier for Chanda than it was for me because nothing intimidates her. She grew up surrounded by confident, self-assured people. Even though Lori and I often played in tournaments held at fancy country clubs, we weren't comfortable in that environment. We weren't used to money and our families weren't used to money.

Chanda climbed to a career high No. 6 after reaching the 1996 Australian Open semifinals. She's extremely intelligent and determined. A wrist injury knocked her out of the top 20, and she has been slow to recover. Eventually, I think she'll work her way back to the top.

Now Venus and Serena Williams, two talented African-American teens from Compton, California, have stormed the tennis world. I nearly missed Serena's victory at the 1999 U.S. Open, but something deep inside told me to catch that plane a day before Serena met Martina Hingis in the final. I'd been Serena's tour-appointed mentor for the previous two years, so I knew I had to be there. I was in the stands, crying like a baby when Serena won 6–3, 7–6 (7–4). My first thought was to call Althea to find out if she had watched the match. We didn't talk, but I left a message on her voice mail. Then I thought about how long it had been since an African-American woman won that Grand Slam title. Althea always said that she would be glad when another black woman won the title so that people would stop asking her about it.

I also thought of the time that Billie Jean King and I spent training Serena on how to hit an underspin backhand. We taught her the shot a couple of months earlier while she and Venus were playing

*Serena and me showing team spirit as part of the U.S. vs. Italy Fed Cup competition in 1999. I was the assistant coach.*

for the U.S. Fed Cup team in Spain. Serena used the backhand under-spin shot several times in the second set when Hingis started rally-ing. Serena plays a solid all-around game steeped in power. She can smack return-of-serve winners from either side, and her own serve is deadly accurate.

After I gave her a congratulatory hug, I took pictures of her hug-ging the trophy. She kept saying, "Zina, Zina, can you believe it, can you believe it? I won, I really won."

Venus was obviously very disappointed. I told her to keep her head up and be happy for her sister. I knew the media would be watching her reaction. Venus said she was happy for Serena but just a little dis-appointed about losing to Hingis 6–1, 4–6, 6–3 in the semifinals.

Venus, who is 6' 2" and laser-quick, won six titles and finished 1999 ranked No. 3 in the world. She has one of the best backhands in the game. Her serve, which frequently is clocked at 120 mph, is a

*Look at the pins I traded with other athletes at the 2000 Olympics.*

major weapon. She used all of her weapons to win Wimbledon 2000, her first Grand Slam title. I have no doubt that she's going to win many more Grand Slam titles.

How can I see these things? Having visions, as you now know, is my special gift.

Venus won the gold medal at the 2000 Sydney Olympics. I was pleased to read an article about her after that which mentioned "a much warmer Venus." She has the image of being arrogant and not wanting to be bothered by people, while Serena is more sociable and outgoing. In reality Venus is pretty shy and veers away because of that. I can relate! It's something we have talked about—letting her personality shine—because she is a wonderful young lady and it's unfortunate that she gets the rap she does sometimes.

The Williams sisters followed my path in another way while in Sydney. In 1988 and '92 I got into pin trading and collecting at the

*Billie Jean King and me at the 2000 Olympics.*

*From the left: me, Monica Seles, and Billie Jean King.*

*From the left: Venus, Serena, and me at the 2000 Olympics.*

Olympic Games. Serena and Venus also became interested in their pin collections and took it to a whole new level! They were trading left and right! It was a nice way for them to socialize with people from other countries in and around Olympic Village. Because tennis is such an individual sport, it doesn't always offer these opportunities to meet people.

Venus signed a multimillion-dollar deal with Reebok a few months before turning pro in 1994. In December of 2000 she signed a $40 million multi-year contract extension with Reebok that was then the most lucrative endorsement deal for a female athlete. Venus said the contract represented a "big moment in my life. Big for women, for people of color, for my whole family. Life has been a dream come true." It's worth noting, too, that Venus' historic moment was made possible by Reebok, the same company that, ten years ago, gave me a barrier breaking multi-year endorsement deal for black women.

Serena, who turned pro in 1997, signed a big-bucks deal with Puma in 1998. There's no question that the Williams sisters already have changed the way people view tennis. Their success is sure to prompt other young black athletes to try tennis. And the best part is that Richard Williams did it his way, without handing the girls over to USTA or academy coaches. People in tennis and the media thought he was crazy, but the man looks more and more like a genius.

I'd like to share one more image from the 2000 Olympics, which I attended with the Williams family. You'll remember that Evonne Goolagong has always been someone I admired and related to as a black person in the sport. And Australia has always been one of my favorite places in the world, from my first visit there many years ago when I learned about the Aborigine culture firsthand. There's American black culture and there's global black culture, with many different faces. Being able to see Australian Cathy Freeman, who is of Aboriginal descent, shine in the 400-meter track event was the epitome of how the Australians welcomed us all to their country. The crowd cheered her as an Australian and allowed her to walk around with the Aborigine flag as well as the Australian national flag. It was amazing and uplifting.

My life right now involves putting together all the experiences that God has allowed me to go through and be able to survive, and to turn the experiences around to help people. The main part of that is to give kids the opportunity to play the game that I love so much. My vision is to have every kid who goes to school at least understand that there is a game called tennis and be able to score it, whether they play it or not. It is a great game, a family sport, and its skills can last a lifetime. If you are lucky like me, what a ride you can go on!

When I first joined the pro tour in 1982, someone asked me how I would like to be remembered when I left the game. I said I wanted to be thought of as a person who cared about other people, gave back, and never forgot her roots. I think I've helped change negative images that some people might have had of players from public parks. I also believe Lori and I broke barriers and made it easier for Katrina Adams, Chanda Rubin, Venus and Serena Williams, and all the other young black women players on the rise. I am pleased and very proud of my accomplishments and my career.

I continue to learn from many people in my life. My supportive family and friends have undoubtedly contributed to the person I have become today, and they continue to be influential. I also must mention Billie Jean King again because she has been an unbelievable source of insight in my life. Her experiences and the battle she has fought for women mean so much to us all. She is always pushing me to be better and to get out there and voice my opinion. She was one of the first people to see beyond my shyness and recognize that I have a lot to say and to give back to the world.

I want to branch out from tennis because it's true that I have so much more to give. It's going to be something with kids, but I have no clue at all as to who it will help and what the ultimate result might be. You don't know who you're tapping and where it's going to go. It could be anything. It could be the whole planet ultimately.

God, thank you for the ride and the dream.

# ZINA GARRISON CAREER HIGHLIGHTS

**Highest Singles Ranking: No. 4**
**Career Prize Money: $4.6 million**

**WTA Tour Singles Titles (14)**

1995: Birmingham, England
1993: Oklahoma City, Budapest
1992: Oklahoma City
1990: Birmingham, England
1989: Oakland, Chicago, Newport
1987: Sydney, San Francisco
1986: Indianapolis
1985: Amelia Island, Fla., European Indoors
1984: European Indoors

**WTA Tour Doubles Titles (20)**

1994: Birmingham, England (with Larisa Neiland)
1993: Chicago (with Katrina Adams), Oklahoma City (with Patty
    Fendick), Zurich (with Martina Navratilova)
1991: Lipton (with Mary Joe Fernandez)
1990: Washington, D.C. (with Navratilova), San Diego (with
    Fendick), Filderstadt, Germany (with M. J. Fernandez)
1989: Houston (with K. Adams), Pan Pacific (with K. Adams),
    Eastbourne, England (with K. Adams)
1988: Tokyo Doubles Championships (with K. Adams), Boca Raton,
    Fla. (with K. Adams), Houston (with K. Adams), Amelia
    Island, Fla. (with Eva Pfaff), Seoul Olympics (with Pam Shriver)
1987: Canadian Open (with Lori McNeil), New Orleans (with L.
    McNeil)
1986: Canadian Open (with Gabriela Sabatini), Indianapolis (with
    L. McNeil)

**Best Results in Grand Slam Singles**

**Australian Open:** semifinalist (1983), quarterfinalist (1985, 87, 89–90)
**French Open:** quarterfinalist (1982)
**Wimbledon:** finalist (1990), semifinalist (1985), quarterfinalist
         (1988, 91, 94)
**U. S. Open:** semifinalist (1988–89), quarterfinalist (1985, 90)

**Best Results in Grand Slam Doubles**

**Australian Open:** finalist (with L. McNeil—1987), finalist (with
         M.J. Fernandez—1992)

**Best Results in Grand Slam Mixed Doubles**

**Australian Open:** champion (with Sherwood Stewart—1989),
         finalist (with Stewart—1989), finalist (with
         Ricky Leach—1990, 1993)
**Wimbledon:** champion (with S. Stewart—1988), champion (with
         R. Leach—1990)

# INDEX